Paul Seligson

with Jane Hudson

ENGLISH FILE
Elementary Workbook without key

Paul Seligson and Clive Oxenden are the original co-authors of
English File 1 and *English File 2*

Contents

1
- 4   A   My name's Hannah, not Anna
- 6   B   All over the world
- 8   C   Open your books, please
- 10   PRACTICAL ENGLISH   Arriving in London

2
- 11   A   A writer's room
- 13   B   Stars and stripes
- 15   C   After 300 metres, turn left

3
- 17   A   Things I love about Britain
- 19   B   Work and play
- 21   C   Love online
- 23   PRACTICAL ENGLISH   Coffee to take away

4
- 24   A   Is she his wife or his sister?
- 26   B   What a life!
- 28   C   Live forever

5
- 30   A   Do you have the X Factor?
- 32   B   Love your neighbours
- 34   C   Sun and the City
- 36   PRACTICAL ENGLISH   In a clothes shop

6
- 37   A   Reading in English
- 39   B   Times we love
- 41   C   Music changes lives

7
- 43   A   At the National Portrait Gallery
- 45   B   Chelsea girls
- 47   C   A night to remember
- 49   PRACTICAL ENGLISH   Getting lost

8
- 50   A   A murder story
- 52   B   A house with a history
- 54   C   A night in a haunted hotel

9
- 56   A   What I ate yesterday
- 58   B   White gold
- 60   C   Quiz night
- 62   PRACTICAL ENGLISH   At a restaurant

10
- 63   A   The most dangerous road…
- 65   B   CouchSurf round the world!
- 67   C   What's going to happen?

11
- 69   A   First impressions
- 71   B   What do you want to do?
- 73   C   Men, women, and the internet
- 75   PRACTICAL ENGLISH   Going home

12
- 76   A   Books and films
- 78   B   I've never been there!
- 80   C   The *English File* questionnaire
- 82   LISTENING

STUDY LINK iChecker

Audio: When you see this symbol *iChecker*, go to the i-Checker disc in the back of this Workbook. Load the disc in your computer.

1

Type your name and press 'ENTER'.

2

Choose 'AUDIO BANK'.

3

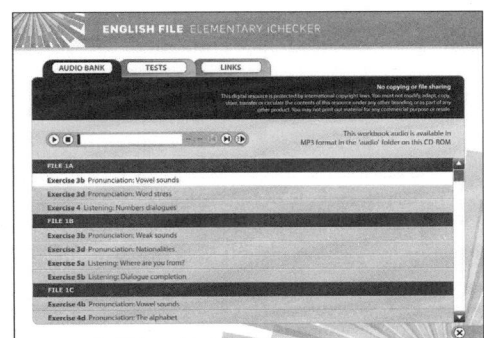

Click on the exercise for the File. Then use the media player to listen.

You can transfer the audio to a mobile device, e.g. your iPod, from the 'audio' folder on the disc.

File test: At the end of every File, there is a test. To do the test, load the i-Checker and select 'Tests'. Select the test for the File you have just finished.

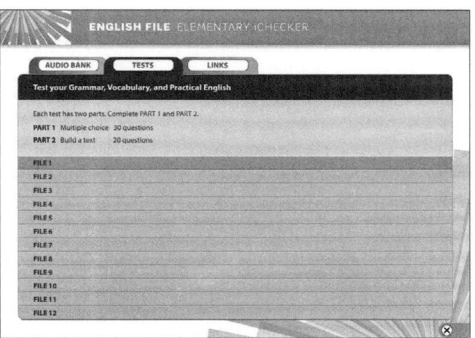

There is also more practice available online at the English File website: www.oup.com/elt/englishfile

No copying or file sharing

This digital resource is protected by international copyright laws. You must not modify, adapt, copy, store, transfer or circulate the contents of this resource under any other branding or as part of any other product. You may not print out material for any commercial purpose or resale.

1A My name's Hannah, not Anna

> My name's Bond. James Bond.
> *Ian Fleming, British writer*

1 GRAMMAR verb be +, subject pronouns

a Complete column 1 with the words in the box. Then write the contractions in column 2.

| she   are   they   is   +   are   is   are |

1 Full form	2 Contraction
I am	1 _I'm_
you 2 _____	3 _____
he 4 _____	5 _____
6 _____ is	7 _____
it 8 _____	9 _____
we 10 _____	11 _____
you 12 _____	13 _____
14 _____ are	15 _____

b Complete the sentences with *be*. Use a contraction.

2 VOCABULARY days of the week, numbers 0–20, greetings

a Put the letters in order to make days of the week. Remember to start with a CAPITAL LETTER.
1 ARSAYDUT   _Saturday_
2 NYAUDS   _____
3 HRDYTUSA   _____
4 ODNYMA   _____
5 DFARYI   _____
6 DSYEEAWND   _____
7 EUASDTY   _____

b Continue the series.
1 five, six, seven, _eight_, _nine_, _ten_.
2 six, eight, ten, _____, _____, _____.
3 twenty, nineteen, _____, _____, _____.
4 five, seven, nine, _____, _____, _____.

1 _I'm_ four.

2 _____ students.

3 _____ in room 2.

4 _____ Thursday.

5 _____ in a taxi.

6 _____ tourists.

7 _____ in room 317.

8 Hello. _____ in my class.

c Complete the dialogues.
1 A Hi, Emily. _This_ is Daniel.
  B Hello, Daniel. _____ to _____ you.
2 A Hi, I'm Pepe. _____'s your _____?
  B Louise.
  A _____?
  B Louise!
3 A Hi, Karl. _____ are you?
  B I'm fine, thanks. And _____?
  A Very well, thank you.
4 A What's your phone _____?
  B It's 07700 900123.

d Complete the words with *a*, *e*, *i*, *o*, or *u*.

1 S_e_ e_ yo_ u.
2 S__ y__ __n Fr__d__y.
3 N__, n__t Fr__d__y. S__t__rd__y!
4 S__rry. S__ y__ __n S__t__rd__y.
5 By__.
6 G__ __dby__.

3 **PRONUNCIATION** vowel sounds, word stress

a Write the words in the chart.

| meet | fine | six | man | ten | eight | three | well | nice |
| in | thanks | day | twelve | very |

ɪ	iː	æ	e	eɪ	aɪ
fish	tree	cat	egg	train	bike

b **iChecker** Listen and check. Then listen again and repeat the words.

c Underline the stressed syllable in these words.
1 sand|wich
2 te|nnis
3 eigh|teen
4 thir|teen
5 bas|ket|ball
6 good|bye
7 e|mail
8 in|ter|net
9 com|pu|ter
10 ho|tel

d **iChecker** Listen and check. Then listen again and repeat the words.

4 **LISTENING**

iChecker Listen to three conversations. Choose a, b, or c.
1 Sarah's phone number is…
   a 161 469 524.
   b 116 496 542.
   c 161 496 542.
2 The class on Thursday is in…
   a room two.
   b room three.
   c room five.
3 A ham sandwich and a coffee cost…
   a five dollars twenty.
   b four dollars twenty.
   c five dollars ten.

USEFUL WORDS AND PHRASES

Learn these words and phrases.
bye /baɪ/
fine /faɪn/
goodbye /ɡʊdˈbaɪ/
hello /həˈləʊ/
hi /haɪ/
sorry /ˈsɒri/
thank you /ˈθæŋk juː/
thanks /θæŋks/
very well /ˈveri wel/
How are you? /haʊ ɑː ˈjuː/
Nice to meet you. /ˈnaɪs tə ˈmiːt juː/

5

> How can you govern a country which has 246 varieties of cheese?
> *Charles de Gaulle, French politician*

1B All over the world

1 GRAMMAR verb *be* ? and −

a Complete B's sentences.

1. **A** Prague is in Hungary.
   B *It isn't in Hungary, it's in* the Czech Republic.
2. **A** Lady Gaga is British.
   B _____ American.
3. **A** He's German.
   B _____ Swiss.
4. **A** Istanbul and Ankara are in Greece.
   B _____ Turkey.
5. **A** We're in room 219.
   B _____ room 309.
6. **A** Parmesan is from France.
   B _____ Italy.
7. **A** You're Brazilian.
   B _____ Argentinian.
8. **A** Enrique Iglesias is American.
   B _____ Spanish.

b Order the words to make questions.

1. your / 's / name / What
   What's your name ?
2. she / Where / 's / from
   _____?
3. America / from / they / South / Are
   _____?
4. five / room / we / in / Are
   _____?
5. holiday / you / Are / on
   _____?
6. from / he / Poland / Is
   _____?

c Match these answers to the questions in **b**.

a Yes, he is. ☐
b No, I'm not. ☐
c She's from Italy. ☐
d No, we aren't. ☐
e Yes, they are. ☐
f Michael. *1*

2 VOCABULARY the world, numbers 21–100

a Complete the sentences with a country or a nationality.

1. Ivana is from Russia. She's _Russian_.
2. Bratwurst is German. It's from _Germany_.
3. Aki is from Japan. He's _____.
4. My friends are Hungarian. They're from _____.
5. Maria is from Mexico. She's _____.
6. Fiat cars are Italian. They're from _____.
7. Paella is from Spain. It's _____.
8. We're Egyptian. We're from _____.
9. She's from the United States. She's _____.
10. They're Brazilian. They're from _____.

b Complete the dialogues with a continent.

1. **A** Where's Spain?
   B It's in _____.
2. **A** Where's Japan?
   B It's in _____.
3. **A** Where's Brazil?
   B It's in _____.
4. **A** Where's Canada?
   B It's in _____.
5. **A** Where's Egypt?
   B It's in _____.

c Complete the compass.

d Write the numbers in words.

1. 27 *twenty-seven*
2. 33 _____
3. 40 _____
4. 48 _____
5. 56 _____
6. 62 _____
7. 74 _____
8. 85 _____
9. 99 _____
10. 100 _____

3 PRONUNCIATION /ə/, /tʃ/, /ʃ/, /dʒ/

a Circle the syllable with /ə/ in these words.

1 A|fri|ca
2 Chi|na
3 Ger|ma|ny
4 Ire|land
5 Eu|rope
6 Po|land
7 I|ta|ly
8 Ja|pan

b **iChecker** Listen and check. Then listen again and repeat the words.

c Circle the word with a different sound.

ʃ shower	1	Poli**sh** Egyp**t**ian Swi**ss**
tʃ chess	2	**Cz**ech English Fren**ch**
ʃ shower	3	Turki**sh** Ru**ss**ian **Ch**inese
dʒ jazz	4	Spani**sh** **J**apanese Ar**g**entinian

d **iChecker** Listen and check. Then listen again and repeat the words.

4 READING

Read about three people: Yin, Moira, and Fadil. Mark the sentences T (true) or F (false).

1 Moira is a teacher. _T_
2 Fadil is a student. __
3 Moira is twenty-eight. __
4 Yin is a teacher. __
5 Yin is from Asia. __
6 Fadil is nineteen. __
7 Yin is twenty-eight. __
8 Moira is British. __

5 LISTENING

iChecker Listen again and complete the dialogues.

1 **A** Are you _____?
   B No, I'm Polish. I'm from Kraków.
2 **A** Where are you from?
   B We're _____. We're from _____. We're on holiday in Europe.
3 **A** Where's he from? Is he _____?
   B No, he isn't. He's _____. He's from Cancún.
4 **A** Mmmm, delicious. Is it _____?
   B No, it isn't. It's _____.

USEFUL WORDS AND PHRASES

Learn these words and phrases.

flag /flæg/
language /ˈlæŋɡwɪdʒ/
Excuse me… /ɪkˈskjuːz miː/
I'm from… /ˈaɪm frɒm/
All over the world. /ɔːl ˈəʊvə ðə ˈwɜːld/
I'm not sure. /aɪm nɒt ʃɔː/
Where are you from? /weə(r) ɑː ju ˈfrɒm/

This is Yin. He's 19 and he's a student. Yin is Chinese. He's from Shanghai, a big city in the East of China.

This is Moira. She's an English teacher and she's 28. Moira is Irish. She's from Galway, a city in the West of Ireland.

This is Fadil. He's Egyptian. He's from Alexandria, an important city in the North of Egypt. Fadil is 25 and he's a receptionist in a hotel.

> Anyone who stops learning is old, whether at twenty or eighty.
> Henry Ford, American businessman

1C Open your books, please

1 GRAMMAR possessive adjectives: *my*, *your*, etc.

a Complete the chart.

Subject pronouns	Possessive adjectives
I	1
2	your
he	3
4	her
5	its
we	6
you	7
8	their

b Complete the sentences with a possessive adjective.
1 _Her_ name's Teresa.
2 _____ name's Edward.
3 We're students. _____ teacher's name is Matt.
4 I'm Irish. _____ family are from Dublin.
5 It's a Chinese restaurant. _____ name is Merry City.
6 A What's _____ phone number?
    B My mobile number? It's 07700 900156.
7 They're Scottish. _____ surname's MacLeod.

c Order the words to make questions.
1 first / her / What's / name
    A _What's her first name_?
    B Sandra.
2 teacher / Where / from / your / 's
    A _____?
    B The United States.
3 he / student / Is / a
    A _____?
    B No, he isn't.
4 you / old / How / are
    A _____?
    B I'm 35.
5 surname / spell / do / How / you / your
    A _____?
    B C-O-O-M-B-S.

2 INSTRUCTIONS IN YOUR BOOK

Match the words to the pictures.

a complete   [3]   f cross   [ ]
b underline   [ ]   g cover the text   [ ]
c match   [ ]   h number   [ ]
d circle   [ ]   i tick   [ ]
e ask your partner [ ] j cross out   [ ]

1 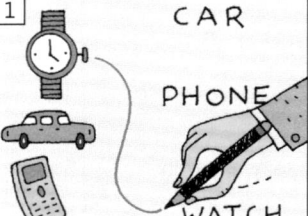 2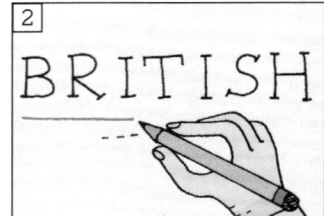
3 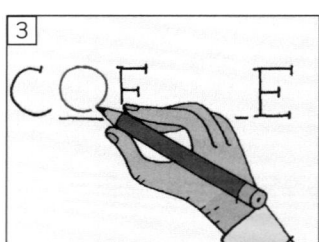 4
5  6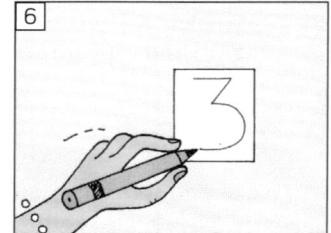
7 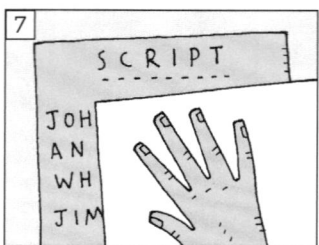 8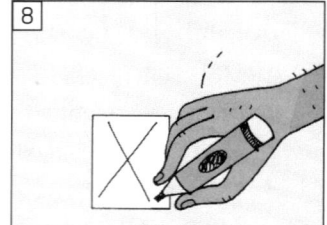
9 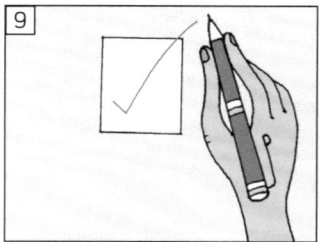 10

3 VOCABULARY classroom language

a Complete the sentences.
1 C*lose* the door.
2 L_____ and repeat.
3 O_____ your books, please.
4 W_____ in pairs.
5 A_____ the question.
6 T_____ off your mobile.
7 L_____ at the board.
8 G_____ to page 94.

b Order the words to make sentences.
1 don't / I / know
   I don't know.
2 do / How / it / you / spell
   _____?
3 don't / I / understand
   _____.
4 you / that / can / please / repeat / Sorry,
   _____?
5 in / English / Excuse / what's / me, / 'vacaciones'
   _____?
6 remember / I / can't
   _____.

4 PRONUNCIATION /əʊ/, /uː/, /ɑː/; the alphabet

a Circle the word with a different vowel sound.

/əʊ/ phone	know	don't	North
/uː/ boot	two	South	you
/ɑː/ car	Asia	France	answer
/əʊ/ phone	go	close	do

b iChecker Listen and check. Then listen again and repeat the words.

c Circle the letter with a different vowel sound.

/eɪ/ train	/iː/ tree	/uː/ boot	/e/ egg	/aɪ/ bike
H J G	C P S	Q U O	F A M	E I Y

d iChecker Listen and check. Then listen again and repeat the letters.

5 LISTENING

iChecker Listen to the dialogue at a hotel reception desk. Complete the form.

First name	1 *Erik*
Surname	2 _____
Country	3 _____
City	4 *Perth*
Address	5 *Atkinson Road*
Postcode	6 _____
Email address	7 _____
Phone number	8 *61*
Mobile number	9 *61*

USEFUL WORDS AND PHRASES

Learn these words and phrases.

address /əˈdres/
age /eɪdʒ/
postcode /ˈpəʊstkəʊd/
receptionist /rɪˈsepʃənɪst/
student /ˈstjuːdnt/
surname /ˈsɜːneɪm/
first name /ˈfɜːst neɪm/
mobile phone /məʊbɪl ˈfəʊn/
phone number /ˈfəʊn nʌmbə/
How old are you? /haʊ ˈəʊld ɑː juː/
I'm 22. /aɪm twenti ˈtuː/

 FILE 1

Practical English Arriving in London

1 VOCABULARY In a hotel

Complete the words.

 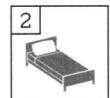 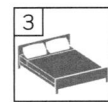   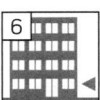

1 the l*ift*_____
2 a s_____ room
3 a d_____ room
4 the b_____
5 r_____
6 the gr_____ fl_____

2 CHECKING IN

Complete the conversation with phrases in the box.

| Can you sign here, please? | I have a reservation |
| Just a second... | Thank you | That's right |

A Good evening, sir.
B Hello. [1] *I have a reservation*. My name's Carl Zimmerman.
A Can you spell that, please?
B Z-I-M-M-E-R-M-A-N.
A Thank you. For three nights?
B Yes. [2] _____.
A Can I have your passport, please?
B [3] _____ Here you are.
A Thank you. [4] _____ Thank you.
  Here's your key. It's room 403, on the fourth floor. The lift is over there. Enjoy your stay, Mr Zimmerman.
B [5] _____.

3 SOCIAL ENGLISH

Complete the missing words in the dialogue.

1 A Who is it?
   B Th*is* is David Barnsley.
2 A Where are you from?
   B I'm from Boston. What a_____ you?
3 A Sorry.
   B No pr_____.
4 A Hello?
   B Is th_____ Tom?
5 A Are you on holiday?
   B No. I'm here on b_____.
6 A Is 10.30 OK for you?
   B That's p_____.
7 A Would you like another drink?
   B No thanks. It's t_____ for bed.

4 READING

a Match the hotels to the people. Write the numbers in the boxes.

1 Antonia and James want to have a relaxing weekend.
2 Mr Edwards wants to have a two-day meeting with managers from other European offices.
3 The Scott family want to go to London and visit the city.

Sheraton Skyline Hotel
Bath Road
Hayes UB3 5BP

- 350 double rooms
- Conference centre
- Restaurants and bar
- Wi-fi connection
- 2 km from Heathrow Airport

The Grove
Chandler's Cross
Hertfordshire WD3 4TG

- 26 suites, 201 luxury rooms
- Room service
- Spa
- Golf course
- Television
- 29 km from Central London

At-Home Bed and Breakfast
20 Denbigh Road Ealing London W13 8QB

- 2 triple rooms, 2 double rooms, and 1 single room
- Garden
- Wi-fi connection
- Television
- Free parking
- Close to central London

b Underline five words or phrases you don't know. Use your dictionary to look up their meaning and pronunciation.

My favourite things in life don't cost any money.
Steve Jobs, American founder of Apple

2A A writer's room

1 VOCABULARY things

Complete the crossword.

2 GRAMMAR a / an, plurals; this / that / these / those

a Write *It's + a / an* or *They're*.

1 *It's a* purse.
2 *They're* pens.
3 _____ diary.
4 _____ umbrella.
5 _____ stamps.
6 _____ keys.
7 _____ identity card.
8 _____ pencil.

b Write each word in its plural form in the correct column.

pencil city coin ticket diary watch window
address sandwich country class dictionary

-s	-es	-ies
coins	addresses	cities

c Complete the sentences with *this*, *that*, *these*, or *those*.

1 *That*'s a French newspaper.

2 _____ watch is Swiss.

3 _____ are my headphones!

4 _____ book is good.

5 _____ are your keys.

11

d Complete the chart.

Singular	Plural
man	
	women
person	
	children

e Complete the sentences with a word from the chart in **d**.
 1 Her mother is a very nice __person__.
 2 My English teacher is a _____. His name's William.
 3 I have two _____. My first _____ is six years old.
 4 Many British _____ drink tea.
 5 Not those toilets, Mr Davis! They're for _____, not _____.

3 PRONUNCIATION final –s and –es; th

a Circle the word which ends in /ɪz/.

 1 coins   wallets   (purses)
 2 classes files   scissors
 3 stamps   books   addresses
 4 photos   watches   headphones
 5 tissues pens   sandwiches
 6 magazines glasses newspapers

b iChecker Listen and check. Then listen again and repeat the words.

c Circle the word with a different sound.

ð mother	1	that	they	thanks
θ thumb	2	thing	thirty	these
ð mother	3	three	this	the
θ thumb	4	Thursday	those	thirteen

d iChecker Listen and check. Then listen again and repeat the words.

4 READING

Read the text and label the pictures.

The top five things in people's bags

Keys are at the top of the list. They can be house keys, car keys, or office keys. Next are pens, to write down names, numbers, and email addresses. Number three on the list is a packet of tissues. These can be white or different colours, like pink or yellow. Next is medicine, for example paracetamol for a bad head. Receipts are number five on the list. These are small pieces of paper from shops.

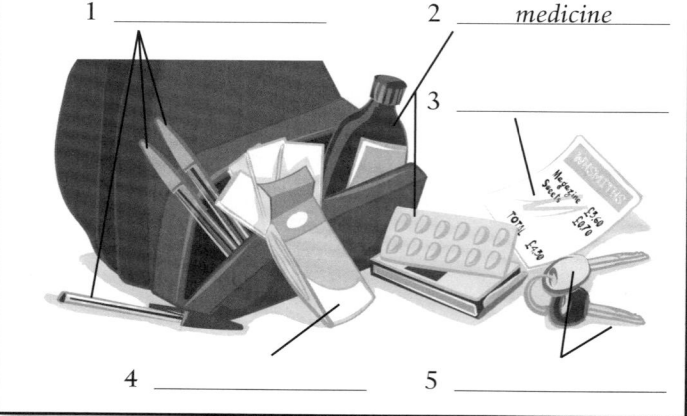

1 _____   2 __medicine__
3 _____
4 _____   5 _____

5 LISTENING

Listen to four people talking about things they have in their bags. Which person…?

 1 has a book in his / her bag which helps him / her speak to people
 2 has something to listen to music
 3 changes bags every day
 4 has a computer in his / her bag

USEFUL WORDS AND PHRASES

Learn these words and phrases.
lamp /læmp/
room /ruːm/
tidy /ˈtaɪdi/
untidy /ʌnˈtaɪdi/
What's this in English? /wɒts ðɪs ɪn ˈɪŋglɪʃ/

2B Stars and stripes

> Not merely a nation, but a nation of nations.
> *Lyndon B Johnson, American president*

1 GRAMMAR adjectives

a Circle the correct words.
1. They're **jeans blue** / **blue jeans**.
2. It's a **nice day** / **day nice**.
3. My sisters are **very tall** / **very talls**.
4. That's a **car fast** / **fast car**.
5. These are **goods photos** / **good photos**.
6. Those boots are **quite cheap** / **quite cheaps**.
7. It's a **big house** / **house big**.
8. Her children aren't **very olds** / **very old**.

b Order the words to make sentences.
1. blue / This / is / a / pen
   This is a blue pen.
2. expensive / an / That's / watch
   _____.
3. quite / My / long / hair / is
   _____.
4. rich / very / is / woman / That
   _____.
5. boots / really / Your / dirty / are
   _____.
6. city / This / a / dangerous / is
   _____.
7. very / book / good / That / isn't / a
   _____.
8. near / house / quite / is / His
   _____.

2 VOCABULARY colours, adjectives, modifiers: *quite / very / really*

a Write the colours.
1. blue + yellow = _green_
2. black + white = _____
3. red + yellow = _____
4. white + red = _____
5. red + green = _____

b Complete the crossword. Write the opposite adjectives.

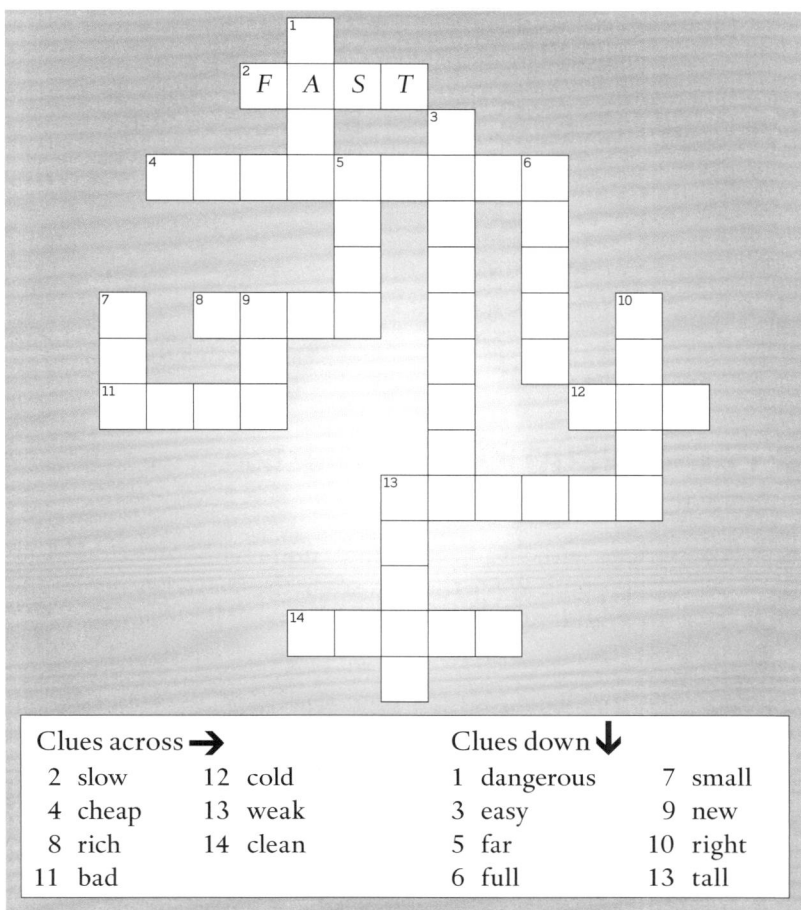

Clues across →
- 2 slow
- 4 cheap
- 8 rich
- 11 bad
- 12 cold
- 13 weak
- 14 clean

Clues down ↓
- 1 dangerous
- 3 easy
- 5 far
- 6 full
- 7 small
- 9 new
- 10 right
- 13 tall

c Match the pictures to the sentences. Write the letter in the box.

1. She's thin, with long hair. **B**
2. He's tall, with short hair. ☐
3. He's quite old, and good-looking. ☐
4. She's young, with blonde hair. ☐
5. He's short, with dark hair. ☐
6. She's quite fat, and she's beautiful. ☐

13

d Look at the information and write sentences with *quite* or *very*.

	Rob	Neil	Jim
Age	15	65	85
Height	2 metres	1 metre 60	1 metre 80
Weight	150 kilos	90 kilos	55 kilos

Age (old / young)
1 Rob is ___quite young___.
2 Neil is quite _____.
3 Jim is _____.

Height (tall / short)
4 Rob _____.
5 Neil _____.
6 Jim _____.

Weight (fat / thin)
7 Rob _____.
8 Neil _____.
9 Jim _____.

3 PRONUNCIATION long and short vowel sounds

a Make phrases with an adjective and a noun with the same vowel sound. Write the phrases in the chart. Use *a / an* with singular nouns.

Adjectives
blue clean dark fat good long big small
Nouns
book city door car jeans man shoes song

fish	1 _a big city_	clock	5 _____
tree	2 _____	horse	6 _____
cat	3 _____	bull	7 _____
car	4 _____	boot	8 _____

b iChecker Listen and check. Then listen again and repeat the words.

4 READING

Read the text and write T (true) or F (false).
1 The Walk of Fame is in the UK. ___
2 It's a short street. ___
3 Every year there are more stars. ___
4 The stars are for famous actors. ___
5 Michael Jackson has more than one star. ___
6 Only real people can have a star. ___

THE HOLLYWOOD WALK OF FAME

Hollywood is a district of Los Angeles in California, USA. The Walk of Fame is in the centre of the district on Hollywood Boulevard and Vine Street. It is over two kilometres long, and has more than 2,400 stars. There are more than 20 new stars every year.

The stars are in five different types: film, TV, music, radio, and theatre. Some famous people have more than one star, for example Michael Jackson. He has two stars: one as a solo artist, and one as a member of the Jackson Five. But the Walk of Fame isn't only for real people. Mickey Mouse has a star and more recently, Shrek.

5 LISTENING

iChecker Listen to five speakers describing celebrities with Hollywood stars. Which speaker describes...?

A a short singer with blonde or brown hair ___
B a quite old American actor with dark eyes ___
C a tall, good-looking man with brown eyes ___
D an actor and musician with blue eyes ___
E a British woman with green eyes ___

USEFUL WORDS AND PHRASES

Learn these words and phrases.
actor /ˈæktə/
actress /ˈæktrəs/
eyes /aɪz/
hair /heə/
musician /mjuˈzɪʃn/
politician /pɒləˈtɪʃn/
sportsman /ˈspɔːtsmən/
sportswoman /ˈspɔːtswʊmən/
singer /ˈsɪŋə/
about (50) /əˈbaʊt/
famous /ˈfeɪməs/
What colour is it? /wɒt ˈkʌlə(r) ɪz ɪt/

> Don't worry, be happy.
> Bobby McFerrin, American musician

2C After 300 metres, turn left

1 GRAMMAR imperatives, let's

a Complete the sentences with a verb in the box. Use a ➕ or a ➖ imperative.

| be | close | come | drink | park | slow | speak | turn | worry |

1 The city is dangerous at night. Please __be__ careful.
2 It's cold in here. Please _____ the window.
3 It isn't a problem. Please _____ about it.
4 This is an English class. Please _____ Spanish.
5 Their house is quite near. Please _____ down.
6 _____ on! We're late!
7 This is a bus stop. Please _____ here.
8 _____ that water – it's dirty.
9 This music is terrible. Please _____ it off.

b Match the sentences to the pictures.

A Let's park here.
B ~~Let's go home.~~
C Let's eat lunch there.
D Let's cross the road here.
E Let's go to a hotel.
F Let's turn on the air conditioning.

1 _B_

2 ___

3 ___

4 ___

5 ___

6 ___

2 VOCABULARY feelings

Write a sentence from the box.

| ~~I'm angry.~~ I'm bored. I'm cold. I'm happy. I'm hot. I'm hungry. I'm sad. I'm stressed. I'm tired. I'm thirsty. I'm worried. |

1 My friend is late.   _I'm angry._
2 It's 3°C.   _____
3 It's my birthday!   _____
4 My mother is in hospital.   _____
5 It's time for dinner.   _____
6 I don't know what to do.   _____
7 It's 42°C.   _____
8 It's very late.   _____
9 My boyfriend is very far away. _____
10 I want a drink.   _____
11 I have a lot of work.   _____

3 PRONUNCIATION understanding connected speech

a Practise saying the sentences.
1 Look at those children.
2 Turn off the TV.
3 Let's ask that man.
4 Don't open the window.
5 Let's eat at home.
6 Sit on this chair.

b **iChecker** Listen and check. Then listen again and repeat the sentences.

15

c Complete the chart with the words in the box.

angry fat happy have hungry matter Monday one
sad ugly worried young

æ cat	ʌ up
angry	

d iChecker Listen and check. Then listen again and repeat the words.

4 READING

a Read the article about tips for a long car journey. Match the headings to the paragraphs.

Have fun!   Is your car ready?   Plan your journey
Make sure everything is in the car   Keep awake!

• **A**   *Plan your journey*
Look at a map before you go. Think about the time you need to arrive at your destination, and places where perhaps there is a lot of traffic.

• **B** _____
Accidents sometime happen because cars are in bad condition. Check the engine, the lights, and the wheels. Take the car to the garage if necessary.

• **C** _____
Put your bags and everything you want to take with you in the hall the night before. Don't forget essential documents like passports or identity cards, and of course your driving licence.

• **D** _____
Being tired is very dangerous for drivers. If you are tired, stop at a service station. Have a coffee, or sleep for 15 minutes. In the car, open the windows and turn the radio on.

• **E** _____
Children are often difficult during long journeys. Take games, for example computer games or word games, and iPods to listen to music. And don't forget things to eat and drink.

b Underline five words you don't know. Use your dictionary to look up their meaning and pronunciation in a dictionary.

5 LISTENING

iChecker Listen to the dialogues and choose a, b, or c.

1 Where are they?
 a at an airport
 b at home
 c in a restaurant
2 Where are they?
 a in a hotel
 b in a car
 c in a restaurant
3 Where are they?
 a in a plane
 b in a hotel
 c in a car
4 Where are they?
 a in a restaurant
 b at home
 c in a car
5 Where are they?
 a in a hotel
 b at an airport
 c at home

USEFUL WORDS AND PHRASES

Learn these words and phrases.

jacket /ˈdʒækɪt/
sign /saɪn/
skirt /skɜːt/
trousers /ˈtraʊzəz/
uniform /ˈjuːnɪfɔːm/
great (*opposite* terrible) /greɪt/
left (*opposite* right) /left/
park (*verb*) /pɑːk/
smoke /sməʊk/
stop /stɒp/
with /wɪθ/
Be quiet! /biː ˈkwaɪət/
Don't worry. /ˈdəʊnt ˈwʌri/
Slow down. /sləʊ ˈdaʊn/
turn on (*opposite* turn off) /ˈtɜːn ɒn/

iChecker TESTS FILE 2

16

3A Things I love about Britain

> Summer afternoon, summer afternoon – the two most beautiful words in the English language.
> *Henry James, American writer who lived in Britain*

1 VOCABULARY verb phrases

Complete the verb phrases.

| animals | dinner | economics | exercise | German |
| glasses | a new car | a newspaper | sorry | an umbrella |

1 cook _____dinner_____
2 study _____
3 speak _____
4 read _____
5 say _____
6 wear _____
7 do _____
8 like _____
9 want _____
10 take _____

2 GRAMMAR present simple + and −

a Circle the correct words.
 1 A lot of British people **drink** / **drinks** tea.
 2 It **don't rain** / **doesn't rain** a lot in my country.
 3 You **live** / **lives** in a beautiful house.
 4 The weather **change** / **changes** quickly in Britain.
 5 My father **don't cook** / **doesn't cook**.
 6 My boyfriend **don't wear** / **doesn't wear** glasses.
 7 People **don't have** / **doesn't have** ID cards in Britain.
 8 We **need** / **needs** a new computer.
 9 My English friend **make** / **makes** good coffee.
 10 I **don't do** / **doesn't do** exercise.

b Look at the chart and complete the sentences.

	Ryan	Kim
eat fast food	✓	✗
wear jeans	✗	✓
drink mineral water	✓	✓
do housework	✓	✗
play the guitar	✗	✗

1 Ryan __eats__ fast food.
2 Ryan _____ jeans.
3 Ryan and Kim _____ mineral water.
4 Kim _____ housework.
5 Ryan and Kim _____ the guitar.
6 Kim _____ fast food.
7 Kim _____ jeans.
8 Ryan _____ housework.

c Complete the sentences.
 1 I __don't play__ (not play) tennis.
 2 They _____ (not go) to the cinema.
 3 She _____ (have) two children.
 4 Her father _____ (not work) in an office.
 5 It _____ (rain) a lot.
 6 We _____ (live) in a big flat.
 7 My girlfriend _____ (not speak) English.
 8 My friends _____ (study) at York University.
 9 You _____ (not do) your homework.

3 PRONUNCIATION vowel sounds, third person -s

a Say the words. Is the vowel sound the same or different? Write **S** (the same) or **D** (different).

 1 say   take   [S]
 2 do   go   [D]
 3 drink live   [ ]
 4 want   have   [ ]
 5 give   drive   [ ]
 6 call   walk   [ ]
 7 read   eat   [ ]
 8 feel   wear   [ ]
 9 play   watch   [ ]
 10 buy   like   [ ]

b **iChecker** Listen and check. Then listen again and repeat the words.

c Circle the word which ends in /ɪz/.
 1 likes   works   **dances**
 2 lives   drinks   watches
 3 drives   finishes plays
 4 uses   takes   speaks
 5 studies listens kisses
 6 changes gives   wears

d **iChecker** Listen and check. Then listen again and repeat the words.

17

4 READING

a Read the text. Match the headings (**A–D**) to the paragraphs.

A A nice cheap place to spend a morning
B Have a nice meal and make new friends
C Yes we can!
D Shopping is so easy

Things I love about the US

Sarah Araf is British but she lives in Ohio, in the US. Here are some things she loves about living there.

1 _____

In the US, the customer is really important. When you walk into a store, the staff greet you with a smile and ask 'How are you?'. The customer is always right too. If you have a problem with something, you take it back and they solve the problem quickly. You don't need to complain. You don't even need to have the receipt.

2 _____

I love real American coffee shops. Not chains like Costa and Starbucks, but those old-fashioned places where the waitresses come to your table and call you 'honey'. You pay a dollar for coffee, and you can drink as much as you like. You can also stay as long as you like. You can sit there all day and read a book for the price of a cup of coffee.

3 _____

Eating out here isn't as expensive as in the UK, so we go out quite a lot. People are very friendly here too. When you go to a bar or a restaurant, you often have a conversation with the people at the next table. It's really nice.

4 _____

Everyone is so optimistic here! They believe that everything is possible if you work hard. If you say 'We can't do that', they say, 'Why not?'!

b Guess the meaning of the highlighted verbs. Check in your dictionary.

5 LISTENING

iChecker Listen to the three speakers talking about Britain. Answer the questions with **H** (Hannah), **A** (Anna), or **R** (Roberta).

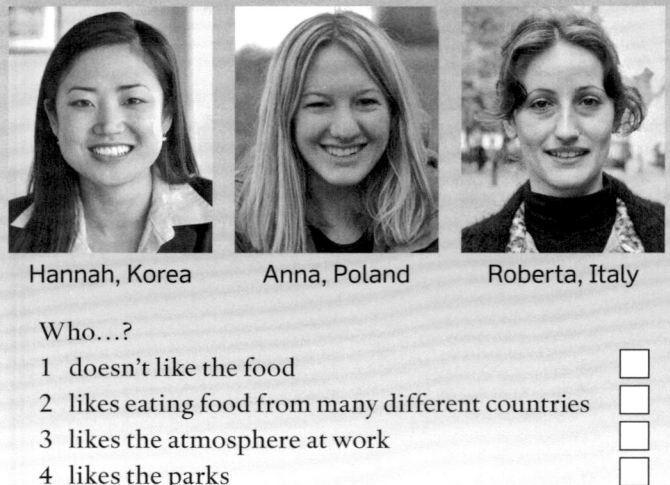

Hannah, Korea   Anna, Poland   Roberta, Italy

Who…?
1 doesn't like the food ☐
2 likes eating food from many different countries ☐
3 likes the atmosphere at work ☐
4 likes the parks ☐
5 thinks the traffic is terrible ☐
6 thinks that people are nice to foreigners ☐

USEFUL WORDS AND PHRASES

Learn these words and phrases.

love /lʌv/
rain /reɪn/
buy (*opposite* sell) /baɪ/
call /kɔːl/
change /tʃeɪndʒ/
feel /fiːl/
need /niːd/
pay /peɪ/
prefer /prɪˈfɜː/

I like to work: it fascinates me.
I can sit and look at it for hours.
Jerome K Jerome, British writer

3B Work and play

1 VOCABULARY jobs

a Complete the crossword.

Clues across →

Clues down ↓

2 E N G I N E E R

b Complete the job descriptions with a verb from the list.

~~work~~ earn speak drive have work travel wear

1 'I [1] _work_ inside and outside during the day or at night.
  I [2] _____ a car and sometimes I walk along the street.
  I don't [3] _____ a lot of money. I [4] _____ a uniform.'

2 'I work in an office with a computer, or outside with other people.
  I [5] _____ French and Spanish and I sometimes
  [6] _____ to different countries. I don't wear a uniform.
  I [7] _____ for a newspaper.'

3 'I wear a uniform and I work with other people. I [8] _____
  special qualifications, but I don't [9] _____ a lot of money.
  I work during the day or at night, but I don't work outside.
  I [10] _____ in a hospital.'

c Match the descriptions to a job.

a journalist ☐   a nurse ☐   a policeman ☐

c Write -er or -or.

1 football*er*
2 manag____
3 administrat____
4 wait____
5 doct____
6 build____

d Complete the sentences with these words.

a an at for in retired unemployed

1 He studies economics _at_ university.
2 My brother is _____ engineer.
3 We work _____ an American company.
4 I don't have a job. I'm _____.
5 Paola is _____ receptionist.
6 My grandparents are 75. They're _____.
7 They work _____ a factory.

19

e Complete the words.

1 j*acket* 2 sh_____ 3 t_____

  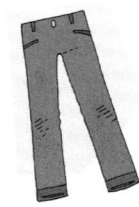

4 sk_____ 5 t_____ 6 tr_____

2 GRAMMAR present simple

a Complete the questions with *Do* or *Does*.

1 __Do__ you work in an office?
2 _____ your parents speak foreign languages?
3 _____ your sister drive?
4 _____ you have special qualifications?
5 _____ your mother work?
6 _____ James travel a lot?
7 _____ your father earn a lot of money?
8 _____ they wear a uniform?
9 _____ Ann walk to work?
10 _____ you work at weekends?

b Complete the questions with *does*, *do*, *is*, or *are*. Then match the questions to the answers.

1 What __does__ she do? [c] a He's an actor.
2 What _____ they do? [ ] b In a restaurant – she's a waitress.
3 _____ he a builder? [ ] c ~~She's a doctor.~~
4 What _____ you do? [ ] d No, they're lawyers.
5 _____ they policemen? [ ] e I'm a hairdresser.
6 Where _____ she work? [ ] f No, he's an engineer.
7 _____ she a student? [ ] g They're pilots.
8 What _____ he do? [ ] h No, she's a teacher.

3 PRONUNCIATION /ɜː/

a Underline the stressed syllable.

1 ad|mi|ni|stra|tor   6 mo|del
2 ar|chi|tect   7 mu|si|cian
3 den|tist   8 pi|lot
4 foot|bal|ler   9 po|lice|man
5 hair|dress|er   10 sol|dier

b **iChecker** Listen and check. Then listen again and repeat the words.

c (Circle) five more words with /ɜː/ and write them in the chart.

doctor (earn) engineer far hairdresser nurse
journalist service short sure thirsty tired
worker worried

/ɜː/ bird	*earn* _____ _____
	_____ _____ _____

d **iChecker** Listen and check. Then listen again and repeat the words.

4 LISTENING

a **iChecker** Listen to a contestant on a quiz show and (circle) his job.

administrator dentist flight attendant
lawyer nurse receptionist vet

b **iChecker** Complete the questions with the verbs in the box. Then listen again and check.

earn have ~~make~~ speak travel wear work

1 __Do you make__ things?
2 _____ special qualifications?
3 _____ foreign languages?
4 _____ a uniform?
5 _____ for your work?
6 _____ a lot of money?
7 _____ with other people?

USEFUL WORDS AND PHRASES

Learn these words and phrases.

jacket /ˈdʒækɪt/
qualifications /ˌkwɒlɪfɪˈkeɪʃnz/
skirt /skɜːt/
trousers /ˈtraʊzəz/
comfortable /ˈkʌmftəbl/
foreign (languages) /ˈfɒrən/
earn money /ɜːn ˈmʌni/
It depends. /ɪt dɪˈpendz/

3C Love online

It's relaxing to go out with my ex-wife because she already knows I'm an idiot.
Warren Thomas, American writer

1 GRAMMAR word order in questions

a Order the words to make questions.
1 heavy / like / you / metal / Do
   Do you like heavy metal?
2 the / do / at / do / What / weekend / you
   _____?
3 kind / What / do / books / read / you / of
   _____?
4 drink / want / another / you / Do
   _____?
5 a / Are / flight / you / attendant
   _____?
6 live / Where / do / Bristol / you / in
   _____?
7 is / favourite / Who / writer / your
   _____?
8 old / How / you / are
   _____?
9 iPad / have / you / an / Do
   _____?
10 your / nice / Is / salad
   _____?

b Martin and Beth are new friends. They go for a drink. Complete the questions.

M So, Beth, ¹ _where do you live_ ?
B In North London. In a big flat.
M ² _____ _____ with your parents?
B No, I live with my sister. ³ _____ _____ _____ any brothers and sisters?
M I have a sister. She's 23.
B ⁴ _____ _____ a student?
M No, she works. She's a shop assistant.
B What about you? ⁵ _____ _____ _____ work?
M In a hotel.
B ⁶ _____ _____ _____ your job?
M Yes, I do. I love it!

2 VOCABULARY question words

Complete the questions with the questions words in the box.

| ~~How~~ How many What What kind When Where Which Who Why |

1 A _How_ do you go to work?
  B By car.
2 A _____ car do you drive?
  B A Mini.
3 A _____ do you work?
  B In a factory.
4 A _____ do you go to the gym?
  B On Tuesdays and Thursdays.
5 A _____ do you prefer, the cinema or the theatre?
  B The theatre, I think.
6 A _____ of music do you like?
  B Rock.
7 A _____ CDs do you have?
  B About a hundred.
8 A _____ is your favourite singer?
  B Rihanna.
9 A _____ do you like her?
  B Because she has a great voice.

3 PRONUNCIATION question words; sentence stress

a Match the question words 1–7 to the words with the same sounds a–g.

1 why   □   a you
2 which   □   b hot
3 who   □   c there
4 what   □   d my
5 how   □   e ten
6 when   □   f rich
7 where   □   g now

b iChecker Listen and check. Then listen again and repeat the words.

21

c Underline the stressed words.

1 A <u>What</u> do you <u>do</u>?
2 B I'm a <u>doctor</u>.
3 A <u>Where</u> do you <u>work</u>?
4 B I <u>work</u> in a <u>hospital</u>.

d **iChecker** Listen and check. Then listen again and repeat the sentences.

4 READING

a Read the article. Is *Facebook* good for your love life? _____

Love on Facebook

Is *Facebook* good for your love life? Read on to find the answer.

1 ☐ C
You don't want to see your ex-boyfriend when your relationship finishes. And you really don't want to know about his new girlfriend. But *Facebook* tells you everything, including how happy he is with his new girlfriend.

2 ☐
Your boyfriend doesn't write on your 'wall' one day. You're worried. Does it mean he doesn't like you? Another day, he sends you ten messages. You feel stressed. Does he like you too much?

3 ☐
Your friends know you have a new boyfriend because you change your status from 'single' to 'in a relationship'. The problem is they know when it finishes too, because you change it back to 'single' again.

4 ☐
You get a lot of messages from boys but this isn't good for your relationship. When your boyfriend sees you writing to so many other boys, he feels worried. And that can mean the beginning of the end.

b Read the article again. Match the headings A–D to the paragraphs 1–4.

A No secrets on *Facebook*
B Popularity is dangerous
C ~~Too much information~~
D What does he *really* feel?

5 LISTENING

a **iChecker** Max and Jessica meet in a restaurant for dinner. Listen to the conversation. Are they a good match? _____

b **iChecker** Listen again and mark the sentences T (true) or F (false).

1 Max and Jessica meet in a Japanese restaurant. *T*
2 They have the same job. ___
3 They work for the same airline. ___
4 They like the same films. ___
5 Jessica lives near the cinema. ___
6 Max wants to go to the cinema next Sunday. ___

USEFUL WORDS AND PHRASES

Learn these words and phrases.

films /fɪlmz/
TV programmes /ˌtiːviː ˈprəʊɡræmz/
Me too. /miː ˈtuː/
meet a partner /miːt ə ˈpɑːtnə/
Really? /ˈrɪəli/
Who's your favourite (actor)? /huːz jɔː ˈfeɪvərɪt/
How interesting! /haʊ ˈɪntrəstɪŋ/
What about you? /wɒt əbaʊt ˈjuː/

iChecker TESTS FILE 3

Practical English Coffee to take away

1 VOCABULARY Telling the time

Write the times.

1 It's half past two. 2 _____ 3 _____ 4 _____

5 _____ 6 _____ 7 _____ 8 _____

2 BUYING A COFFEE

Order the dialogue.

1	A	Can I help you?
	B	No thanks. How much is that?
	A	Anything else?
	B	Thanks.
	A	£3.65. Thank you. And your change.
	B	Sorry, how much?
	A	Regular or large?
2	B	Yes. Can I have a latte, please?
	A	That's £3.65, please.
	B	To take away.
	A	To have here or take away?
	B	Large, please.

3 SOCIAL ENGLISH PHRASES

Complete the sentences with the words in the box.

| a seat | first time | to drink | to you | ~~we are~~ |

1 Here _we are_. This is the office.
2 Is this your _____ in the UK?
3 Would you like something _____?
4 Talk _____ later.
5 Take _____.

4 READING

a Read about some coffee bars in Edinburgh. In which bar can you…?
1 find a lot of sweet food
2 sit in the same place as a famous person
3 have a coffee in the evening
4 take your coffee to your office
5 find somewhere for small children to sit

A URBAN ANGEL 121 Hanover Street
Urban Angel is open every day for breakfast and brunch, coffee and cake, lunch and dinner. If you don't want to sit down and eat, you can pay less and take your food out. The food is healthy and there are tables inside and outside.

B THE ELEPHANT HOUSE 21 George IV Bridge
This coffee bar is popular with tourists because J K Rowling started writing the Harry Potter books here. It serves excellent coffee, and you can see the collection of big and small elephants while you are there. There is also a selection of snacks.

C TWO THIN LADDIES 103 High Riggs
A very friendly family runs this café and the homemade food is delicious. It's a very calm and relaxing place, and it's also very private. Vegetarian food is available, and there are high chairs for children.

D CHOCO-LATTE 33–39 South Clerk Street
This is actually a sweet shop with a small area at the back for customers to drink coffee. They sell amazing sweets and cakes, and there's chocolate everywhere. It's ideal for birthdays and everything is quite cheap.

E KILIMANJARO COFFEE 104 Nicolson Street
This coffee bar serves some of the best coffee in Edinburgh. It opens later than most other cafés, and it's always busy. There's a comfortable couch and a lot of tables and chairs. The food is also fantastic.

b Guess the meaning of the highlighted food words. Check the meaning and pronunciation in your dictionary.

4A Is she his wife or his sister?

> A celebrity is a person who works hard all his life to become well-known, then wears dark glasses to avoid being recognized.
> *Fred Allen, American comedian*

1 VOCABULARY family

a Complete the chart.

¹ *grandmother*	grandfather
mother	²
³	uncle
wife	⁴
⁵	brother
daughter	⁶
⁷	nephew
cousin	⁸

b Complete the sentences.
1 My father's brother is my *uncle* .
2 My sister's daughter is my _____.
3 My mother's sister is my _____.
4 My father's mother is my _____.
5 My aunt's daughter is my _____.
6 My brother's son is my _____.

2 GRAMMAR *Whose...?*, possessive *'s*

a Order the words to make sentences.
1 in / work / father's / my / shop / I
   I work in my father's shop .
2 German / boyfriend's / My / car / is
   _____.
3 girlfriend's / is / His / Polish / mum
   _____.
4 Sandra's / Do / know / you / brother
   _____?
5 live / wife's / with / parents / my / We
   _____.
6 of / money / earns / friend / son's / a / Their / lot
   _____.
7 dangerous / Is / job / Adam's
   _____?
8 uniform / very / Susan's / ugly / is
   _____.

b Add an apostrophe (') in the correct place in these sentences.
1 Martha is my brother's girlfriend.
2 That is my parents car.
3 I think this is that womans pen.
4 They drink tea in the Teachers Room.
5 Do you know Barbaras sister?
6 My grandparents house is in Ireland.
7 Richards wife is Russian.

c Look at the *'s* in these sentences. Write a letter in the box:
A = possessive, **B** = *is*.
1 Kate's sister is a lawyer. [A]
2 His mother's very short. [B]
3 My cousin's flat is very big. ☐
4 Our grandfather's 70 today. ☐
5 Their uncle's a pilot. ☐
6 Jim's children wear glasses. ☐
7 My brother's wife plays the piano. ☐
8 Her name's Christina. ☐

d Complete the sentences with *whose* or *who's*.
1 *Whose* is that bag?
2 *Who's* the woman in the red dress?
3 _____ umbrella is this?
4 _____ her boyfriend?
5 _____ the man with the sunglasses?
6 _____ are those keys?
7 _____ your English teacher?
8 _____ headphones are those?

3 PRONUNCIATION the letter o; 's

a Match the sentences 1–4 to the sounds a–d.

1	Those mobile phones are old.	☐	a	↑ up
2	Who do you choose?	☐	b	əʊ phone
3	Their son comes every Monday.	☐	c	ɒ clock
4	That blonde model is a doctor.	☐	d	uː boot

b **iChecker** Listen and check. Then listen again and repeat the words.

c **iChecker** Listen to the sentences. Then listen again and repeat.

1 /s/ That's Mark's niece.   They're Kate's parents.

2 /z/ He's Sandra's husband.   She's Andy's cousin.

3 /ɪz/ I'm Grace's boyfriend.   Are you Charles's wife?

4 READING

a Read the article and complete the sentence.

Liam Neeson is Vanessa Redgrave's _____.

An acting family

The Redgrave family is one of the most famous acting families in the UK. Vanessa Redgrave is probably the most famous of them.

Vanessa's parents, Michael and Rachel, were both actors and her grandparents, Roy and Daisy, were actors, too. Vanessa's first husband was the actor Tony Richardson and they had two daughters, Natasha and Joely. Vanessa and Tony were divorced, and later Vanessa married again. Vanessa's second husband was the Italian actor, Franco Nero, and together they had a son called Carlo.

Vanessa's first daughter, Natasha, married actor Liam Neeson in 1994. Together they had two sons Micheál and Daniel. Unfortunately, Natasha died in a skiing accident in 2009.

Vanessa's other daughter, Joely, married film producer Tim Bevan. Together they have a daughter, Daisy.

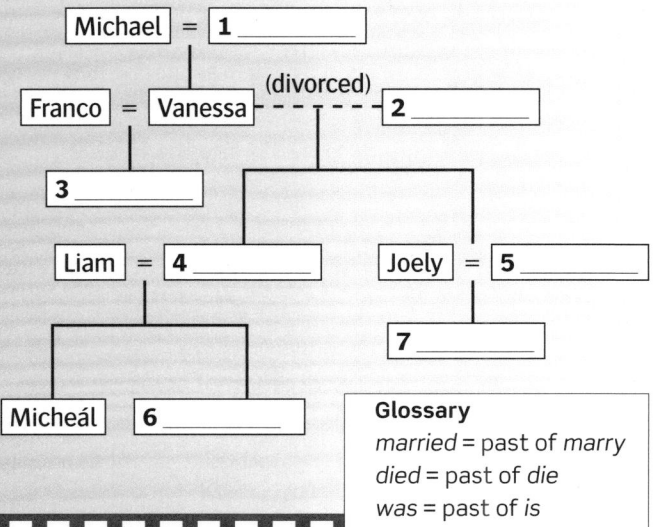

Glossary
married = past of marry
died = past of die
was = past of is
were = past of are
had = past of have

b Read the article again and complete the names in the family tree.

5 LISTENING

iChecker Listen to Jessie showing photos to her friend. How many photos does she show? Then listen again. Write T (true) or F (false).

1 Jessie's sister has a son.   _F_
2 Jessie's sister is short.   ___
3 Jessie's sister plays basketball.   ___
4 The beach in the photo is in Germany.   ___
5 Jessie went to a music festival with her sister.   ___
6 Rosie has blonde hair.   ___
7 Rosie sees her boyfriend all the time.   ___
8 Pete is Jessie's boss.   ___

USEFUL WORDS AND PHRASES

Learn these words and phrases.

boyfriend /ˈbɔɪfrend/
celebrity /səˈlebrəti/
ex-husband /eks ˈhʌzbənd/
girlfriend /ˈɡɜːlfrend/
royalty /ˈrɔɪəlti/
be interested in /bi ˈɪntrestɪd ɪn/
private life /ˈpraɪvət laɪf/
the other (person) /ði ˈʌðə/

25

4B What a life!

3 o'clock is always too late or too early for anything you want to do.

Jean-Paul Sartre, French philosopher

1 GRAMMAR prepositions of time (*at, in, on*) and place (*at, in, to*)

a Write the words in the correct column.

March 6th December 6.30 the winter Monday night the afternoon the weekend Saturday evening 1984 Christmas 21st August

in	on	at
March	6th December	6.30

b Circle the correct preposition.
1 I have a shower **in** / **on** / **at** the morning.
2 They go on holiday **in** / **on** / **at** August.
3 My sister studies economics **at** / **in** / **to** university.
4 My brother goes to bed **in** / **on** / **at** midnight.
5 Do you work **at** / **in** / **to** a hospital?
6 We have English classes **in** / **on** / **at** Tuesdays and Thursdays.
7 The children have lunch **at** / **in** / **to** school.
8 Tina works **in** / **on** / **at** the weekend.
9 Jack goes **at** / **in** / **to** the gym after work.
10 It's very hot **in** / **on** / **at** the summer.

c Complete the text with the correct prepositions.

'My name is Francesco Mancini and I work ¹_____ an office in the centre of Rome. During the week, I get up ²_____ half past six. I go ³_____ work by train, but ⁴_____ Fridays I drive my car so I can visit my mother ⁵_____ the afternoon. I start work ⁶_____ quarter to nine and I have lunch ⁷_____ work. ⁸_____ the summer I work different hours because ⁹_____ 15th June we change to the summer timetable. It's very hot in Rome ¹⁰_____ August, so most people go on holiday.

2 VOCABULARY everyday activities

a Circle the action which you usually do first.
1 get up / (wake up)
2 get dressed / have a shower
3 have lunch / have breakfast
4 go to work / start work
5 go home / get home
6 make the dinner / go shopping

b Complete the text with *have*, *go*, or *get*.

A STUDENT'S LIFE IS EASY – OR IS IT?

Many people think that students have a very easy life. We ask two, Helen and Rupert, about their typical day.

HELEN EDWARDS, from Durham in north-east England

'I ¹ _go_ to university in Bristol, so I don't live at home. Every day, I ²_____ up at 7.30 and I ³_____ a shower. I don't have time for breakfast, but I ⁴_____ coffee in a café before classes start. I ⁵_____ lunch at university and then I ⁶_____ to my afternoon classes. I ⁷_____ shopping on my way home, so I ⁸_____ home late. I do some housework and study in the evening and then I ⁹_____ to bed at 11.30. I'm very tired at night!'

RUPERT CAVENDISH is from Exeter in south-west England

'I ¹⁰_____ to Exeter University, so I live at home. My mum wakes me up every morning and we ¹¹_____ breakfast together. Then, I ¹²_____ dressed. I ¹³_____ to university by bus. I ¹⁴_____ to classes in the morning and then I ¹⁵_____ home for lunch. My mum is a good cook and we ¹⁶_____ lunch together. In the afternoon, I study for an hour or two and then I watch TV. I ¹⁷_____ a bath after dinner. I'm quite relaxed when I ¹⁸_____ to bed.'

26

c Match the words to make phrases.
   1 have   a work
   2 go   b emails
   3 check   c dressed
   4 do   d to school
   5 get   e breakfast

3 PRONUNCIATION linking and sentence stress

a Mark the connected words in each sentence.
   1 You get up late.
   2 I have a shower.
   3 We check emails.
   4 He does exercise.
   5 She goes home early.
   6 They have lunch at work.

b iChecker Listen and check. Then listen again and repeat the sentences. Try to connect words.

c iChecker Listen and <u>underline</u> the stressed words. Copy the <u>rhy</u>thm.
   1 I wake up at six.
   2 I have a coffee.
   3 I go to work by bus.
   4 I do the housework.
   5 I have a pizza for dinner.
   6 I go to bed at midnight.

d iChecker Listen again and repeat the sentences. Copy the <u>rhy</u>thm.

4 LISTENING

a iChecker Listen to an interview with Mark. Answer the questions.
   1 What does he do? _____
   2 Does he like his job? _____
   3 When does he work? _____

b iChecker Listen again. Number the activities in the order Mark does them.
   [1] Mark starts work at 7 p.m.
   [ ] He goes to bed.
   [ ] He goes to the gym.
   [ ] He goes home.
   [ ] He has a hamburger or a pizza.
   [ ] He watches TV or checks his emails.
   [ ] He gets up.
   [ ] He has breakfast.
   [ ] He sleeps for eight hours.
   [ ] He has dinner.
   [ ] He finishes work.
   [ ] He has a shower.

USEFUL WORDS AND PHRASES

Learn these words and phrases.

customers /ˈkʌstəməz/
everyone /ˈevriwʌn/
everything /ˈevriθɪŋ/
menu /ˈmenjuː/
busy /ˈbɪzi/
ready /ˈredi/
a couple of (hours) /ə ˈkʌpl əv/
go back /ɡəʊ ˈbæk/
prepare food /prɪ peə ˈfuːd/
enjoy /ɪnˈdʒɔɪ/

> The man who works and is not bored is never old.
> *Pablo Casals, Spanish cellist*

4C Live forever

1 GRAMMAR position of adverbs and expressions of frequency

a Complete the *You* column in the chart. Then complete the sentences with a verb and an adverb of frequency.

		Matt	Becky	You
always	✓✓✓✓✓			
usually	✓✓✓✓			
often	✓✓✓			
sometimes	✓✓			
hardly ever	✓			
never	–			
sleep for eight hours		✓✓✓✓	✓✓	
be relaxed		✓✓✓✓✓	✓✓✓	
do sport or exercise		✓✓	–	
eat healthy food		✓✓✓	✓	
be ill		–	✓✓✓✓✓	

1 Matt _usually sleeps_ for eight hours.
2 He _____ relaxed.
3 He _____ sport or exercise.
4 He _____ healthy food.
5 He _____ ill.
6 Becky _____ for eight hours.
7 She _____ relaxed.
8 She _____ sport or exercise.
9 She _____ healthy food.
10 She _____ ill.
11 I _____ for eight hours.
12 I _____ relaxed.
13 I _____ sport or exercise.
14 I _____ healthy food.
15 I _____ ill.

b Write the adverb of frequency in the correct place in the sentence.

1 Pilots sleep in hotels. (often)
   Pilots often sleep in hotels .
2 The children walk to school. (every day)
   The children walk to school every day. .
3 Mike rides his motorbike to work. (sometimes)
   _____.
4 My girlfriend is late. (never)
   _____.
5 I see my grandparents. (every weekend)
   _____.
6 Ellie drinks coffee. (three times a day)
   _____.
7 I'm hungry. (always)
   _____.
8 We study English. (twice a week)
   _____.

2 VOCABULARY adverbs and expressions of frequency

a Answer the questions.

THE TIME QUIZ

1 How many minutes in an hour? _____
2 How many months in a year? _____
3 How many days in a week? _____
4 How many seconds in a minute? _____
5 How many weeks in a month? _____
6 How many hours in a day? _____
7 How many days in June? _____
8 How many weeks in a year? _____

b Complete the sentences with one or two words.

1 Leo goes to the gym all week and at weekends.
  Leo goes to the gym _every_ _day_ .
2 Jon usually has a holiday in the summer and winter.
  Jon usually has a holiday _____ a year.
3 We usually see one new film a month.
  We go to the cinema _____ a month.
4 Adele doesn't do any homework at all.
  Adele _____ does homework.
5 They have English classes on Mondays, Wednesdays, and Fridays.
  They have English classes _____ _____ a week.
6 My mother goes to the hairdresser once a week, on a Friday.
  My mother goes to the hairdresser _____ Friday.
7 Eve walks to work once a year.
  Eve _____ ever walks to work.
8 I always buy a new pair of sunglasses in the summer.
  I buy a new pair of sunglasses _____ summer.

28

3 PRONUNCIATION the letter h

a Match the words to their pronunciation. In which word is the *h* not pronounced? _____

1 half — e — a /hɪə/
2 high — □ — b /ˈaʊə/
3 how — □ — c /haɪ/
4 hour — □ — d /ˈhʌri/
5 hardly — □ — e /hɑːf/
6 here — □ — f /ˈhæpi/
7 hurry — □ — g /ˈhɑːdli/
8 happy — □ — h /haʊ/

b **iChecker** Listen and check. Then listen again and repeat the words.

4 READING

a Read the interview. What is surprising about Esther Armstrong?

Interview with
Esther Armstrong, 94

Interviewer	How do you spend your day, Esther?
Esther	My day is very normal, really. I get up, I get dressed, I have breakfast. Then I go to work.
Interviewer	What do you do?
Esther	I'm an accountant.
Interviewer	Why do you still work, Esther?
Esther	To have an interest. Also, my job is quite exciting.
Interviewer	What time do you start work?
Esther	I start between 9 and 10 every day and I finish at 4 o'clock. It isn't very stressful, really.
Interviewer	What do you usually do after work, Esther?
Esther	I go out for dinner with friends two or three times a week, and we go to the cinema or the theatre, or to the ballet.
Interviewer	Do you live alone?
Esther	Yes, I do. I have quite a big apartment and someone helps me with the housework for four hours a week. I do everything else myself.
Interviewer	Do you have children, Esther?
Esther	Yes, I do. Both of my daughters live here in New York. One daughter works very near, and she comes and has lunch with me. And I work with the other daughter, so we eat together two or three times a week, too. I'm very, very happy with my life.

Glossary
an accountant = a person whose job it is to make lists of all the money that people or businesses receive and pay

b Read the interview again. Write T (true) or F (false).
1 Esther thinks her day is normal. _F_
2 She doesn't like her job. __
3 She sometimes starts work at 10 o'clock. __
4 She thinks her job is difficult. __
5 She often sees friends after work. __
6 She lives with one of her children. __
7 She never does housework. __
8 She has two children. __

c <u>Underline</u> five words you don't know. Use your dictionary to look up their meaning and pronunciation.

5 LISTENING

a **iChecker** Listen to a radio programme about being healthy. Who does the doctor say is healthy: Marge, Robbie, or Marge and Robbie?
_____

b **iChecker** Listen again. Write T (true) or F (false).
1 Robbie doesn't think he's healthy. _F_
2 Marge hardly ever eats fast food. __
3 Marge always has breakfast. __
4 Marge often goes to the gym. __
5 Marge goes to bed late. __
6 Robbie sometimes has breakfast. __
7 Robbie plays football three times a week. __
8 Robbie sleeps for six hours every night. __

USEFUL WORDS AND PHRASES

Learn these words and phrases.

hours /ˈaʊəz/
minutes /ˈmɪnɪts/
seconds /ˈsekəndz/
teenager /ˈtiːneɪdʒə/
healthy (*opposite* unhealthy) /ˈhelθi/
normally /ˈnɔːməli/
relax /rɪˈlæks/
be in a hurry /biː ɪn ə ˈhʌri/
social life /ˈsəʊʃl laɪf/
spend time /spend ˈtaɪm/

iChecker TESTS FILE 4

> In the future everyone will be famous for fifteen minutes.
>
> Andy Warhol, American painter

5A Do you have the X factor?

1 GRAMMAR can / can't

a Write a sentence for each picture with *can / can't*.

1 *They can't sing* .

2 _____ .

3 _____ .

4 _____ .

5 _____ .

b Write a question with *you* for each picture. Then write your answer: *Yes, I can.* or *No, I can't.*

Your answer

1 *Can* you *sing* ? _____ .
2 _____ you _____ ? _____ .
3 _____ you _____ ? _____ .
4 _____ you _____ ? _____ .
5 _____ you _____ ? _____ .

c Match sentences 1–6 to a–f.

1 Can you help me with my homework? I [c]
2 Can you give me my glasses? I [   ]
3 Can you call my mum? I [   ]
4 Can you speak more slowly? I [   ]
5 Can you make dinner for 8.30? I [   ]
6 Can you tell me your name again? I [   ]

a can't come before then.
b can't see.
c ~~can't do it.~~
d can't find my mobile.
e can't understand you.
f can't remember it.

d Write a sentence with *can* or *can't* for each picture.

1 You *can cross* now.

2 I _____ now.

3 Dr Atkins _____ you now.

4 We _____ here!

2 VOCABULARY verb phrases

a Complete the crossword with the correct verb.

b Complete the sentences.

| buy | find | hear | help | look for | play | run | talk |

1. He can't _find_ any parking spaces. There are a lot of cars.
2. I often _____ chess with my nephew. He's very good.
3. Please _____ me. I can't open the door.
4. I _____ most of my clothes from Zara.
5. I want to _____ in the London Marathon this year.
6. Hi, this is Paul. Can you _____ me?
7. I don't understand this. I need to _____ to the teacher.
8. Where are my keys? Can you _____ them?

3 PRONUNCIATION sentence stress

a iChecker Listen and repeat the sentences. Stress the **bold** words.

1. A **Can** you **speak German**?
   B **Yes**, I **can**.
2. I **can't find** the **keys**.
3. **She** can **sing**.
4. **Where** can I **buy** a **newspaper**?
5. A **Can** your **father cook**?
   B **No**, he **can't**.
6. My **sister can't swim**.

b Write the words in the chart.

| bad | bath | can | can't | class | dance | fat |
| have | stamp | start |

æ cat	_bad_	_____	_____
	_____	_____	_____
ɑː car	_bath_	_____	_____
	_____	_____	_____

c iChecker Listen and check. Then listen again and repeat the words.

4 LISTENING

iChecker Listen to the dialogues and choose a, b, or c.

1. When can they go to the swimming pool?
   a On Saturday morning.
   b On Saturday afternoon.
   c On Sunday afternoon.
2. Where can the man park?
   a Outside the hospital.
   b Outside the restaurant.
   c Outside the cinema.
3. When can she help her brother?
   a This morning.
   b This afternoon.
   c This evening.
4. Why can't they send the postcard?
   a They don't have a pen.
   b They don't have the address.
   c They don't have a stamp.
5. Why can't they go in?
   a She can't open the door.
   b She can hear her parents.
   c She can't find her keys.

USEFUL WORDS AND PHRASES

Learn these words and phrases.

audience /'ɔːdiəns/
concerts /'kɒnsəts/
entrance /'entrəns/
judges /'dʒʌdʒɪz/
late (*opposite* early) /leɪt/
nervous /'nɜːvəs/
a hit record /ə hɪt 'rekɔːd/
car park /'kɑː pɑːk/
Good luck! /gʊd 'lʌk/
It's your turn now. /ɪts 'jɔː tɜːn naʊ/

31

> Hell is other people.
> Jean-Paul Sartre, French philosopher

5B Love your neighbours

1 VOCABULARY verb phrases

Complete the text with these verbs in the present simple.

| argue shout bark cry talk have |
| have play play |

My neighbours are very noisy. A young couple with a baby and a dog live upstairs. They aren't happy together so they ¹ *shout* all the time. Their dog ² _____ when they aren't at home, and their baby ³ _____ when they are. An old couple live downstairs. They can't hear so they always ⁴ _____ the TV on very loud. They ⁵ _____ loudly because the TV is loud, and they ⁶ _____ a lot about which programmes to watch. Some students live next door. They all ⁷ _____ musical instruments and they aren't very good! Every night, they ⁸ _____ noisy parties and ⁹ _____ very loud music. I want a new flat or some new neighbours!

2 GRAMMAR present continuous

a Order the words to make sentences.
1 sister's / My / exams / for / studying / her.
   My sister's studying for her exams.
2 with / staying / week / her / friends / this / are / Sarah's
   _____.
3 tonight / party / We / a / aren't / having
   _____.
4 I'm / cup / coffee / drinking / a / the / of / kitchen / in
   _____.
5 for / looking / job / is / a / George / Why
   _____?
6 because / aren't / They / jogging / today / cold / it's / too
   _____.
7 computer / Are / using / you / the
   _____?
8 football / Is / park / Adam / playing / in / the
   _____?

b Complete the dialogue.

A What ¹ *are you doing*, (you / do) Andy?
B ² _____ (I / make) the coffee. Why?
A I can hear a noise. It's people's voices.
B I know. That's the couple upstairs.
A ³ _____ (they / argue)?
B No, ⁴ _____ (they / not shout). It's the TV. They're very old, so they can't hear it. ⁵ _____ (they / watch) a film.
A Oh. What's that music? Is it a party?
B It's the boy next door. ⁶ _____ (he / not have) a party! ⁷ _____ (he / listen) to music. He likes heavy metal.
A Your flat is very noisy, Andy.
B I know. ⁸ _____ (I / look for) a new one!

c Look at the picture on page 33. What are the people doing? Complete 1–9 with a verb or verb phrase in the present continuous.
1 The woman*'s talking on her mobile.*
2 The couple _____
3 The children _____
4 The woman _____
5 The baby _____
6 The dog _____
7 The boy _____
8 The girl _____

3 PRONUNCIATION /ŋ/

a **iChecker** Listen and repeat the words.

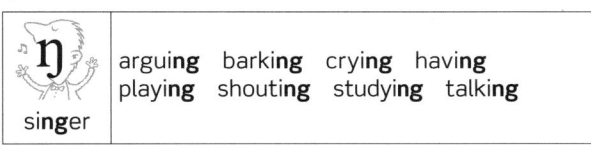

| ŋ singer | arguing barking crying having playing shouting studying talking |

b Circle the word with /ŋ/ in each pair.

1	sing	dance
2	pink	brown
3	thin	long
4	aunt	uncle
5	drink	find
6	France	Hungary
7	young	blonde
8	think	want

c **iChecker** Listen and check. Then listen again and repeat the words.

4 LISTENING

iChecker Listen to four speakers talking about problems with their neighbours. Match the speakers to the problems. There are two problems you don't need to use.

Speaker 1 ☐
Speaker 2 ☐
Speaker 3 ☐
Speaker 4 ☐

A They argue a lot.
B Their dogs bark.
C They have noisy parties.
D They have the TV on very loud.
E Their baby cries.
F They play musical instruments.

USEFUL WORDS AND PHRASES

Learn these words and phrases.

furniture /ˈfɜːnɪtʃə/
neighbours /ˈneɪbəz/
noise /nɔɪz/
noisy /ˈnɔɪzi/
strict /strɪkt/
upstairs (*opposite* downstairs) /ʌpˈsteəz/
now /naʊ/
complain /kəmˈpleɪn/
block of flats /blɒk əv ˈflæts/
washing machine /ˈwɒʃɪŋ məʃiːn/

> I'm leaving because the weather is too good.
> I hate London when it's not raining.
>
> Groucho Marx, American actor

5C Sun and the City

1 GRAMMAR present simple or present continuous?

a Circle the correct form.

1. **A** What are you doing here?
   B I'm on holiday. **I sightsee** / **(I'm sightseeing)**.
2. **A** Can you talk?
   B No. **I have dinner** / **I'm having dinner** at the moment.
3. **A** Where **do they usually go** / **are they usually going** on holiday?
   B To Ibiza.
4. **A** How often does your boyfriend go abroad?
   B **He travels** / **He's travelling** to Asia four times a year.
5. **A** What **does your girlfriend do** / **is your girlfriend doing**?
   B She's a travel guide.
6. **A** **Do you work** / **Are you working** this week?
   B No. I'm on holiday.
7. **A** What time does the museum close?
   B **It closes** / **It's closing** at 6 p.m., I think.
8. **A** **Does it rain** / **Is it raining** today?
   B No. It's hot and sunny.

b Complete the sentences. Use the present simple or present continuous.

1. My parents _don't like_ (not like) their hotel.
2. They _____ (argue) about money all the time.
3. I'm 18 now so I _____ (learn) to drive. My father _____ (teach) me.
4. When _____ you usually _____ (go) to the gym?
5. My brother _____ (go out) nearly every night.
6. The sun _____ (not shine) today. It's quite cold.
7. _____ you _____ (use) your computer at the moment? I _____ (want) to check something on the internet.
8. My sister _____ (love) ice skating but she _____ (not do) it very often.

2 VOCABULARY the weather and seasons

a Write the seasons in the correct order.

winter , _____ , _____ , _____

b Complete the sentences with words in the box. What's the weather like?

cloudy   cold   foggy   hot   raining   snowing   sunny   windy

1 It's _hot_ .

2 It's _____ .

3 It's _____ .

4 It's _____ .

5 It's _____ .

6 It's _____ .

7 It's _____ .

8 It's _____ .

3 PRONUNCIATION places in London

a Underline the stressed syllable.

1 Buck|ing|ham Pa|lace
2 West|min|ster A|bbey
3 Ox|ford Street
4 St Paul's Ca|the|dral
5 Pi|cca|di|lly Cir|cus
6 Lei|cester Square
7 Hou|ses of Par|lia|ment
8 Tra|fal|gar Square

b **iChecker** Listen and check. Then listen again and repeat the words.

4 READING

Read the guidebook extract about things to do in Edinburgh. Write T (true) or F (false).

1 Edinburgh Castle is outside the city.   _F_
2 You can see some important things from Scotland's past in the castle.   ___
3 You can't see the city from the castle.   ___
4 Arthur's Seat is outside Edinburgh.   ___
5 You don't need to be fit to walk to the top of Arthur's Seat.   ___
6 You can see the city very well from the top.   ___
7 Scottish people have a special name for New Year.   ___
8 You can't buy things to eat at the street party.   ___
9 Every year, people sing a different song at New Year.   ___

5 LISTENING

iChecker Listen to the audio guide on a tour bus in Dublin and write the number of the stop.

At which bus stop do you need to get off if you want to…?

A see some famous paintings   ☐
B learn about a famous drink   ☐
C read a letter from a famous writer   ☐
D see a lot of books   _1_
E relax and listen to music   ☐
F visit an important historical building   ☐
G learn about life in a prison   ☐
H see some animals   ☐

What to do in EDINBURGH...

1 WHEN IT'S RAINING Go to Edinburgh Castle

Edinburgh Castle is a very old building, high on a hill in the centre of Edinburgh. You can take a tour of the castle or walk around on your own. You can see many interesting exhibitions, including the Scottish Kings and Queens of the past, and the National War Museum. If the sun comes out, you have a fantastic view of the shops and buildings on Edinburgh's famous street, the Royal Mile.

2 WHEN THE SUN IS SHINING Go to Arthur's Seat

Arthur's Seat is a high hill in the centre of Edinburgh with excellent views of the city. You can choose an easy walk or a difficult walk to the top, depending on how fit you are. From the top you can see all of Edinburgh's famous monuments including the Castle, the Royal Mile, and Holyrood Palace. It's the perfect place to take some great photos of the city.

3 WHEN IT'S COLD Go to Princes Street at New Year

New Year has a different name in Scotland: Hogmanay – and the Hogmanay Party in Princes Street – is famous all over the world. Over four days, thousands of people join in the fun in the street, and you can buy hot food and drinks all night. At midnight, everyone sings a traditional New Year's song called *Auld Lang Syne*, and then they watch some fantastic fireworks from Edinburgh Castle.

USEFUL WORDS AND PHRASES

Learn these words and phrases.

building /ˈbɪldɪŋ/
guidebook /ˈɡaɪdbʊk/
monument /ˈmɒnjumənt/
parks /pɑːks/
statue /ˈstætʃuː/
enormous /ɪˈnɔːməs/
fascinating /ˈfæsɪneɪtɪŋ/
wonderful /ˈwʌndəfl/
including /ɪnˈkluːdɪŋ/
open-air swimming pool /ˌəʊpən eə ˈswɪmɪŋ puːl/

iChecker TESTS FILE 5

Practical English In a clothes shop

1 VOCABULARY clothes

Write the words.

1 _a jacket_
2 _____
3 _____
4 _____
5 _____
6 _____
7 _____
8 _____

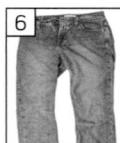

2 BUYING CLOTHES

Complete the missing words in the dialogue.

A Can I ¹h__ you?
B Yes. What ²s_____ is this T-shirt?
A It's a medium. What size do you need?
B I need a ³l_____.
A Here you ⁴a_____.
B Thanks. Where can I try it on?
A The ⁵c_____ rooms are over there.
B ⁶Th_____ you.
A How is it?
B It's fine. How ⁷m_____ is it?
A It's 15.99.

3 SOCIAL ENGLISH

Match the words to make Social English phrases.

1 It's so   [d]   a way!
2 Right   [ ]   b wrong?
3 Don't   [ ]   c be silly!
4 Wait   [ ]   d cool!
5 I have to   [ ]   e fun!
6 Have   [ ]   f now.
7 What's   [ ]   g go.
8 No   [ ]   h a minute.

4 READING

a Read the article. Match the questions A–D to paragraphs 1–4.

A What can you do there?   [1]
B How do you get there?   [ ]
C Where can you eat?   [ ]
D What time does it open? [ ]

Shopping in the UK

One of the best places to shop in the UK these days is at the Westfield Stratford City shopping centre in London – the biggest and newest of its kind in Europe.

1 Customers at Westfield can buy fashion, food, home, and beauty products from more than 300 different stores. There are two huge department stores and a large supermarket. It has a 14-screen cinema and a bowling alley, and there are also two hotels and a casino.

2 Inside the shopping centre, there are 72 different restaurants and food bars. There are takeaways and sit-down restaurants, including Halal and vegetarian cake shops and salad bars. Many of the bars and restaurants stay open after the shops close.

3 Most of the stores in the shopping centre open from 10 a.m. to 9 p.m. during the week, and from 9 a.m. to 9 p.m. on Saturday. The opening hours on Sunday are from 11 a.m. to 5 p.m. The restaurants close at around midnight and the cinema closes at 1 a.m., except on Saturdays when it closes at 2 a.m.

4 Westfield has 5,000 parking spaces and it is very easy to get to on public transport. Two underground lines connect the shopping centre to Central London, and there are many buses. Westfield is only eight minutes from Liverpool Street station by train.

b Guess the meaning of the highlighted words. Check the meaning and pronunciation in your dictionary.

6A Reading in English

> Reading is a basic tool in the living of a good life.
> Joseph Addison, British writer and politician

1 GRAMMAR object pronouns

a Complete the chart.

Subject pronouns	Object pronouns
I	¹me
²	you
he	³
she	⁴
⁵	it
we	⁶
⁷	you
they	⁸

b Complete the sentences with object pronouns.

1 My sister has a new boyfriend. She's on holiday with _him_ at the moment.
2 Can you hear _____, or do I need to shout?
3 This book is very exciting. I'm really enjoying _____.
4 He works near his wife's office. He has lunch with _____ every day.
5 Are you at home? Can I call _____ later?
6 Harry doesn't live with his parents, but he speaks to _____ once a week.
7 Excuse me, we have a problem. Can you help _____?
8 I can't find my bag. Can you see _____?
9 These shoes are new. Do you like _____?
10 Where's Charlie? I want to talk to _____.

c Complete the text with these words.

| he | her | her | ~~him~~ | him | she | them | they |

Lily is worried about her boyfriend, Jamie. She calls ¹ _him_ every day, but he doesn't call ² _____. When she wants to talk to Jamie ³ _____ always says he's busy. She waits for ⁴ _____ after work, but he's often with some friends. Jamie's friends don't like Lily, and she doesn't like ⁵ _____. Lily says hello, but ⁶ _____ don't look at her. Now she knows that Jamie doesn't love ⁷ _____. But she's happy because she knows that ⁸ _____ can find a new boyfriend.

2 VOCABULARY phone language

Complete the dialogues with these words.

| answer | It's | message |
| Press | ~~there~~ | this | wrong |

1 A Hello. Is Millie __there__?
  B No, I'm sorry. She isn't.
2 A What number is that?
  B _____ 07723 9832.
3 A The phone's ringing.
  B Can you _____ it, please?
4 A Hello, is that Sophie?
  B No, I'm sorry, _____ is Grace.
5 A How do I finish this call?
  B _____ the red button.
6 A This is 0454 93822.
  B I'm very sorry. It's the _____ number.
7 A I'm sorry, the manager is in a meeting.
  B Oh. Can you give him a _____?

3 PRONUNCIATION /aɪ/, /ɪ/, and /iː/

a **iChecker** Listen and repeat the sentences. Stress the **bold** words.

1 **Call** me **tonight**.
2 **Can** you **help** us?
3 **Don't listen** to **her**.
4 **See** you **later**.
5 **I don't like** them.
6 **Don't think** about it.
7 **Give it** to **him**.

b Circle the word with a different sound.

fish	1 him live nice	fish	4 these his ring
tree	2 she this meet	tree	5 we leave it
bike	3 me I my	bike	6 smile niece buy

c iChecker Listen and check. Then listen and repeat the words.

4 READING

Read some more of *Sally's Phone* and answer the questions.

1 Who's Katharine? _____
2 What does Louise suggest to Sally? _____
3 Why doesn't Paul know his phone number? _____
4 Who tells him what his number is? _____

Sally's Phone

Sally talks to Claire and Louise.
  'I've got a message for Paul – but who's Paul? Do you know a Paul, Claire?' she asks.
  'No. What's the message?' Claire asks.
  'It's his sister Katharine's birthday, and she's having a party tonight. Do you think it's a wrong number?'
  'Yes, I think it is,' Claire says.
  'Hey, Sally!' Louise says. 'Put on your red skirt and go to the party. Forget Andrew!'
Paul talks to a friend at work.
  'This is Sally's phone – and Sally's got my phone.'
  'But who is Sally?'
  'I don't know,' says Paul.
  'Why don't you phone her?'
  'What's my number?' Paul asks. 'I don't know my number.'
  'Why not?'
  'Because I never call my number!'
Paul phones his mother.
  'Mum, what's the number of my phone?'
  'Why do you want your phone number, Paul?'
  'Because Sally's got my phone.'
  'Who's Sally?' his mother asks.
  'I don't know, but she's got my phone, and I've got her phone.'
  'I don't understand.'
  'I know,' says Paul. 'It doesn't matter. Have you got my number?'
  'Here it is. 0781 644834.'
  'Thanks, Mum.'

Glossary
I've got = I have
She's got = She has

5 LISTENING

iChecker Listen to the phone conversation. Choose a or b.

1 Who does Holly want to talk to?
  a Beth   b Emily
2 Where is Emily?
  a at home   b out
3 Where is Holly's bag?
  a in Emily's car   b in Emily's house
4 What is Holly's phone number?
  a 60674 923   b 60674 823
5 What does Beth give Emily?
  a the message   b the phone
6 Which keys are in Holly's bag?
  a her car keys   b her flat keys
7 Who is Holly with?
  a a neighbour   b a friend
8 Where do Holly and Emily meet?
  a at Holly's house   b in a café

USEFUL WORDS AND PHRASES

Learn these words and phrases.

voice /vɔɪs/
fall /fɔːl/
happening /ˈhæpənɪŋ/
ring /rɪŋ/
smile /smaɪl/
give a message (to somebody) /gɪv ə ˈmesɪdʒ/
pick up /ˈpɪk ʌp/
press the button /pres ðə ˈbʌtn/
put down /ˈpʊt daʊn/
It's the wrong number. /ɪts ðə rɒŋ ˈnʌmbə(r)/

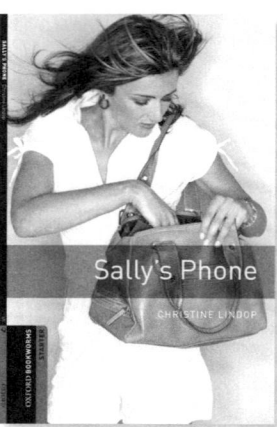

Extract from Oxford Bookworms Library Starter:
Sally's Phone by Christine Lindop © Oxford University Press 2008.
Reproduced by Permission.
ISBN 978-0-19-423426-9

6B Times we love

If we had no winter, the spring would not be so pleasant.
Ann Bradstreet, American poet

1 GRAMMAR like (+ verb + -ing)

a Write the verb + *-ing* form of the verbs in the box in the correct column.

<del>buy</del> come draw find get have give run stop swim take wait

verb + -ing	e + -ing	double consonant + -ing
buying		

b Look at the chart and complete the sentences.

☺☺ = love
☺ = like
😐 = don't mind
☹ = don't like
☹☹ = hate

	William	Amanda
dance at parties	☹☹	☺☺
do housework	😐	☹☹
drive at night	☺	☹
sit in cafés	😐	☺
swim in the sea	☺☺	☹
watch football	☹	☺☺

1 William *hates dancing* at parties.
  Amanda _____ at parties.
2 William _____ housework.
  Amanda _____ housework.
3 William _____ at night.
  Amanda _____ at night.
4 William _____ in cafés.
  Amanda _____ in cafés.
5 William _____ in the sea.
  Amanda _____ in the sea.
6 William _____ football.
  Amanda _____ football.

2 VOCABULARY the date; ordinal numbers

a Continue the series.
  1 September, October, *November*, *December*
  2 May, June, _____, _____
  3 January, February, _____, _____
  4 spring, summer, _____, _____
  5 first, second, _____, _____
  6 sixth, seventh, _____, _____
  7 eighteenth, nineteenth, _____, _____

b Complete the chart.

1/1   14/2   4/7   31/10   <del>25/12</del>

Day	Date	You say...
Christmas Day	25/12	*the twenty-fifth of December*
Halloween		
New Year's Day		
US Independence Day		
Valentine's Day		

3 PRONUNCIATION consonant clusters; saying the date

a Under<u>line</u> the stressed syllable in the multisyllable words.
  1 <u>Ja</u>nuary   7 July
  2 February   8 August
  3 March   9 September
  4 April   10 October
  5 May   11 November
  6 June   12 December

b **iChecker** Listen and check. Then listen and repeat the words.

39

c **iChecker** Listen and repeat the dates.

1	3 / 4	6	14 / 6
2	26 / 12	7	1 / 2
3	11 / 5	8	7 / 11
4	5 / 1	9	22 / 10
5	18 / 3	10	12 / 7

4 READING

Read the article about important dates in the UK and find the answers to the questions. Write **A**, **B**, **C**, or **D**.

On which day or days…?
1 do some people watch football on TV — C
2 do people remember a moment in history
3 do people celebrate a change in the weather
4 do people go to work
5 do people hear stories which aren't true
6 do some people wear special clothes

UK dates to remember

A April Fool's Day is on 1st April. It isn't a public holiday, but it's a day when people play jokes on friends and family. Some good jokes are in the newspapers or on TV – for example, one year on the BBC there was a programme about spaghetti trees in Switzerland. Many people believed it was true!

B In most countries, **May Day** is on 1st May, but in the UK the holiday is always the first Monday of May. A traditional May Day activity is maypole dancing, when people in colourful clothes dance around a tree or a pole to celebrate the end of winter and the start of sunny weather.

C Boxing Day is a holiday on 26th December. If this is a weekend, then the holiday is the following Monday. The name comes from the custom of giving servants a small box with a present or money on this day. Some families meet to watch sport, while others prefer to go shopping on the first day of the sales.

D Bonfire Night isn't a holiday but it is a national celebration. On 5th November, people remember Guy Fawkes' plan to destroy the English Parliament in 1605. The plan was not a success, and every year since then towns and villages have huge bonfires and fantastic firework displays. They also burn a model of the man responsible for the plan: Guy Fawkes.

5 LISTENING

a **iChecker** Listen to four speakers talk about their favourite times of year. Match the speakers to the seasons.

Speaker 1   spring
Speaker 2   autumn
Speaker 3   winter
Speaker 4   summer

b **iChecker** Listen again. Match the speakers to the activities they enjoy doing at that time of year.

Speaker 1 ☐
Speaker 2 ☐
Speaker 3 ☐
Speaker 4 ☐

a walking
b planning
c taking photos
d travelling

USEFUL WORDS AND PHRASES

Learn these words and phrases.

Easter   /ˈiːstə/
asleep   /əˈsliːp/
depressing   /dɪˈpresɪŋ/
outside (*opposite* inside)   /aʊtˈsaɪd/
hate   /heɪt/
in a good mood   /ɪn ə ɡʊd ˈmuːd/
When's your birthday?   /wenz jɔː ˈbɜːθdeɪ/

> Ah, music. A magic beyond all we do here!
>
> *J K Rowling, British author*

6C Music changes lives

1 GRAMMAR revision: *be* or *do*?

a Complete the sentences with the correct form of *be* or *do*.

1 What __are__ you listening to?
2 Which instrument _____ you play?
3 The singer _____ Spanish. She's Argentinian.
4 I _____ buy CDs. All my music is on my iPod.
5 We _____ watching a film. We're watching the news.
6 _____ your boyfriend like reggae?
7 Which song _____ your brother downloading?
8 He _____ sing in a group. He's a solo artist.
9 They _____ go to concerts because it's too expensive.
10 _____ you a member of a fan club?

b Rewrite the sentences as questions.

1 They listen to music online.
   Do they listen to music online?
2 Adam sings karaoke.
   _____?
3 She's singing in the shower.
   _____?
4 That guitar's expensive.
   _____?
5 They go to a lot of musicals.
   _____?
6 I'm waiting in the right place.
   _____?
7 Kathy likes reggae.
   _____?
8 You go dancing at the weekend.
   _____?
9 He listens to classical music when he's stressed.
   _____?
10 They're in an orchestra.
   _____?

2 VOCABULARY music

a Complete the words.

1 Rihanna is an R_&_B singer from Barbados.
2 Kings of Leon are an American **r**_____ band.
3 Black Eyed Peas are a famous **h**_____ **h**_____ group.
4 Iron Maiden are an English **h**_____ **m**_____ band.
5 John Lee Hooker is famous for **b**_____ music.
6 Bach and Beethoven are two German composers of **c**_____ **m**_____.
7 Jennifer Lopez is a popular singer of **L**_____ music.
8 Many **r**_____ musicians are from Jamaica.
9 Jamie Cullum plays modern **j**_____.

41

b Complete the sentences with the words in the box.

concert   go dancing   download   fan club
karaoke   lyrics   music channels   online

1 My friends and I often _go dancing_ on a Saturday night.
2 My sister loves Green Day and she's a member of their _____.
3 I _____ new music onto my MP3 player nearly every day.
4 My children love watching _____, especially MTV.
5 When she's using her laptop, she often listens to music _____.
6 I like the song, but I don't understand the _____.
7 Many Japanese people love singing _____.
8 Would you like to come to a _____ tonight? I have two tickets for Leonard Cohen.

3 PRONUNCIATION /j/

a Circle the word which doesn't have /j/.

	j yacht	
1 use	beautiful	umbrella
2 young	journalist	yellow
3 nurse	new	music
4 musician	lunch	usually
5 January	student	summer

b iChecker Listen and check. Then listen and repeat the words.

4 LISTENING

iChecker Listen to the dialogues and choose a, b, or c.
1 Oliver thinks reggae is…
  a loud.
  b slow.
  c great.
2 The people who sing on the woman's favourite CD are…
  a a classical choir.
  b a rock band.
  c actors.
3 Wendy usually listens to music…
  a online.
  b on CDs.
  c on the radio.
4 The second man really likes…
  a Rihanna.
  b Beyoncé.
  c Justin Bieber.
5 John…the song.
  a likes
  b doesn't mind
  c hates

USEFUL WORDS AND PHRASES

Learn these words and phrases.

a band /ə bænd/
conductor /kən'dʌktə/
karaoke /kæri'əʊki/
orchestra /'ɔːkɪstrə/
soundtrack /'saʊndtræk/
awful /'ɔːfl/
fantastic /fæn'tæstɪk/
be a fan (of…) /bi ə 'fæn (ɒv)/
Be a member (of…) /bi ə 'membə/
download music /'daʊnləʊd 'mjuːzɪk/
go dancing /gəʊ 'dɑːnsɪŋ/

iChecker TESTS FILE 6

> My life is a simple thing that would interest nobody.
> It is a known fact that I was born, and that is all that is necessary.
>
> Albert Einstein, German scientist

7A At the National Portrait Gallery

1 GRAMMAR past simple of be: was / were

a Complete the sentences with *was*, *were*, *wasn't*, or *weren't*.

A Who's that?
B It's Jane Austen.
A Why [1] _was_ she famous?
B She [2] _____ a writer.
A [3] _____ she Scottish?
B No, she [4] _____.
She [5] _____ English. She [6] _____ born in a small village in the South of England.
A And [7] _____ she married?
B No, she [8] _____.

b Write questions and answers.

1 Alexander Graham Bell / sportsman? ✗
  Was Alexander Graham Bell a sportsman ?
  No, he wasn't .

2 Richard Burton and Elizabeth Taylor / actors? ✓
  Were Richard Burton and Elizabeth Taylor actors ?
  Yes, they were .

3 Charles Dickens / novelist? ✓
  _____?
  _____.

4 The Beatles / from the USA? ✗
  _____?
  _____.

5 Lord Byron / politician? ✗
  _____?
  _____.

6 Isaac Newton / composer? ✗
  _____?
  _____.

7 Bono / born / Ireland? ✓
  _____?
  _____.

8 Amy Winehouse / singer? ✓
  _____?
  _____.

9 J R R Tolkien and C S Lewis / painters? ✗
  _____?
  _____.

10 Michael Jackson / born / Britain? ✗
  _____?
  _____.

c Complete the dialogues with present or past forms of *be*.

1 A What day _is_ it today?
  B Monday. Yesterday _was_ Sunday.

2 A Hi. _____ your sister at home?
  B No, she _____. She _____ here this morning, but now she _____ at work.

3 A I can't find my keys. Where _____ they?
  B I don't know. They _____ on your desk this morning.

4 A Where _____ your new boyfriend from?
  B He _____ born in England, but his parents _____ born in Singapore.

5 A Why _____ your boss angry yesterday?
  B Because I _____ very late for work.

43

2 VOCABULARY word formation

a Make professions from these words. Use *a* or *an*.

1 invent — *an inventor*
2 write — _____
3 police — _____
4 compose — _____
5 music — _____
6 paint — _____
7 business — _____
8 act — _____
9 science — _____
10 sail — _____

b Un<u>der</u>line the stressed syllables, e.g. *an in<u>ven</u>tor*.

c Practise saying the words in **a**.

d Complete the sentences with *was / were* and a noun from **a**.

1 Francis Drake _was a sailor_.
2 Beethoven and Mozart _were composers_.
3 James Dean _____.
4 Galileo _____.
5 Freddie Mercury _____.
6 The Wright brothers _____.
7 Agatha Christie _____.
8 Howard Hughes _____.
9 Degas and Toulouse-Lautrec _____.

3 PRONUNCIATION sentence stress

iChecker Listen and repeat the conversation.

A Who was Benjamin Britten?
B He was a composer.
A Was he American?
B No, he wasn't. He was English.
A When was he born?
B He was born in 1913.
A Were his parents English?
B Yes, they were.

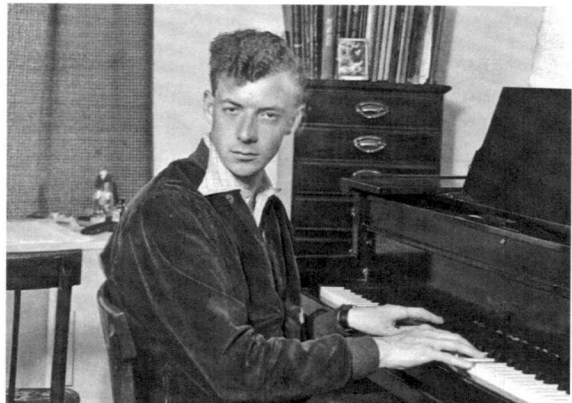

4 LISTENING

a **iChecker** Listen to a radio programme about the greatest Britons of all time. Number the people in the order they come on the list.

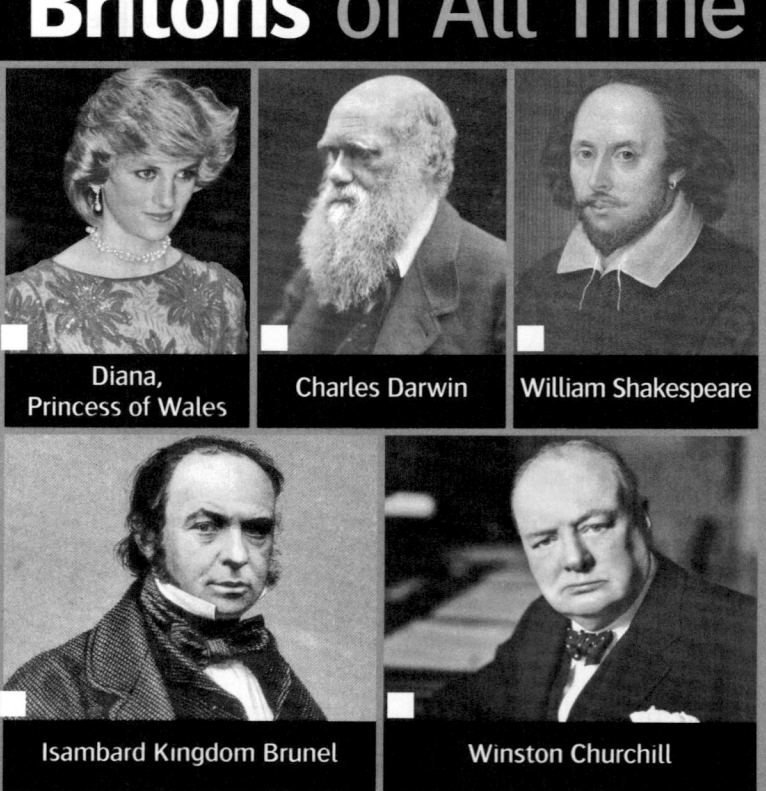

b **iChecker** Listen again. Write T (true) or F (false).

1 We don't know when Shakespeare was born. _T_
2 Charles Darwin was born on 20th February, 1809. ___
3 He was 63 when he died. ___
4 Diana was born on 1st July, 1961. ___
5 She wasn't married when she died. ___
6 Isambard Kingdom Brunel was a writer. ___
7 He was 53 when he died. ___
8 The greatest Briton of all time was a painter. ___

USEFUL WORDS AND PHRASES

Learn these words and phrases.

the (16th) century /ðə ˈsentʃəri/
divorced /dɪˈvɔːst/
between (1816 and 1820) /bɪˈtwiːn/
be against (something) /bi əˈɡeɪnst/
be in love (with someone) /bi ɪn ˈlʌv/

44

> I kissed my first woman and smoked my first cigarette on the same day. I never had time for tobacco after that.
>
> Arturo Toscanini, Italian conductor

7B Chelsea girls

1 GRAMMAR past simple: regular verbs

a Complete the sentences with a regular verb in the past simple, first in the positive and then in the negative.

book   download   listen   ~~miss~~   play   study   watch   work

1 Yesterday I _missed_ my bus, but I _didn't miss_ my train.
2 We _____ to the news, but we _____ to the weather.
3 My parents _____ French at school, but they _____ Spanish or Italian.
4 My sister _____ the film with me, but she _____ the football match.
5 The secretary _____ a table for lunch, but she _____ a taxi.
6 I _____ some music onto my laptop, but I _____ any films.
7 The shop assistant _____ last Saturday, but she _____ on Sunday.
8 My boyfriend _____ rugby at school, but he _____ basketball.

b Order the words to make questions.

1 you / did / night / TV / What / on / last / watch?
   A _What did you watch on TV last night_?
   B I watched the news.
2 did / match / the / time / finish / What
   A _____?
   B At six o'clock.
3 your / presents / birthday / like / you / Did
   A _____?
   B Yes, I did. They were great!
4 did / university / your / at / brother / What / study
   A _____?
   B Modern Languages.
5 parents / your / arrive / late / Did
   A _____?
   B No, they didn't. They were early.
6 Germany / your / in / friends / did / Where / live
   A _____?
   B Hamburg.
7 of / you / Did / at / the / cry / film / end / the
   A _____?
   B Yes, I did. It was very sad.
8 time / work / did / What / arrive / Sandra / yesterday / at
   A _____?
   B At ten o'clock.

c Complete the questions and answers.

1990   ~~1994~~   1997   2001   2004   2007   2009

When did it happen?

1 when / the Channel Tunnel / open
   When did the Channel Tunnel open?
   It opened in _1994_.

2 when / Michael Jackson / die
   _____?
   He died in _____.

3 when / Facebook / start
   _____?
   It started in _____.

4 when / Princess Diana / die
   _____?
   She died in _____.

5 when / the first tourist / travel into space
   _____?
   The first tourist travelled into space in _____.

6 when / iPhones / first appear
   _____?
   They appeared in _____.

7 when / Tim Berners-Lee / create the World Wide Web
   _____?
   He created it in _____.

2 VOCABULARY past time expressions

Circle the correct answer.

1. I chatted to my friends for an hour **last night** / **yesterday night**.
2. My girlfriend finished university **ago two years** / **two years ago**.
3. They travelled abroad **last month** / **the last month**.
4. Did you call me **last morning** / **yesterday morning**?
5. It stopped raining **two hours ago** / **two ago hours**.
6. My brother worked in Greece **last July** / **the last July**.
7. We watched that film **before two weeks** / **two weeks ago**.
8. David booked the tickets **yesterday afternoon** / **last afternoon**.
9. Steve was born **in 1990** / **on 1990**.
10. I played golf **the day yesterday before** / **the day before yesterday**.

3 PRONUNCIATION -ed endings

a **iChecker** Listen to the words. Underline the word where -ed is pronounced /ɪd/.

1 booked	checked	wanted	walked
2 painted	arrived	finished	travelled
3 asked	waited	looked	stopped
4 called	played	chatted	listened
5 missed	watched	cooked	started
6 followed	decided	lived	relaxed

b Listen again and repeat the words.

4 READING

a Read the article and choose the best title.

1. The wrong match
2. The wrong destination
3. The wrong player

b Read the article again and answer the questions.

1. How old was Bojana when the incident happened?
2. Where was the tennis tournament?
3. How did she travel to Carlsbad?
4. Where did Bojana travel to first?
5. When did she arrive at the tournament?
6. Who did she play in her first match?
7. Did she win?

5 LISTENING

a **iChecker** Listen to four speakers describing bad journeys. How did they travel (e.g. by car, etc.)?

1. _____
2. _____
3. _____
4. _____

b **iChecker** Listen again and match the speakers 1–4 to the sentences a–d.

Speaker 1 ☐
Speaker 2 ☐
Speaker 3 ☐
Speaker 4 ☐

A A stranger helped me.
B Someone in my family helped me.
C I started my journey twice.
D I didn't arrive at my destination.

USEFUL WORDS AND PHRASES

Learn these words and phrases.

satnav /ˈsætnæv/
surprised /səˈpraɪzd/
arrive /əˈraɪv/
cry /kraɪ/
miss /mɪs/
text /tekst/
travel /ˈtrævl/
country house /ˌkʌntri ˈhaʊs/

Serbian tennis player Bojana Jovanovski was only 19 when she played in the San Diego Open. However, she very nearly missed the tournament. Her first match was in Carlsbad, California, so her agent booked a seat for her and gave her the ticket to Carlsbad. It was a long journey because Bojana needed to take three different planes. When she finally arrived in Carlsbad, she was surprised to find that the airport was empty. She waited for 15 minutes and then called Tournament Transport. The problem was that Bojana was in Carlsbad, New Mexico and the transport service was in Carlsbad, California where the tournament was. So, Bojana stayed in New Mexico for the night and then travelled to Carlsbad, California the next morning. She arrived only 30 minutes before the start of her match with the Italian player Roberta Vinci. Unfortunately, the day finished badly for Bojana because she lost the match 3-6, 6-4, 6-1. After that, she just wanted to go home!

7C A night to remember

> Never be the first to arrive at a party or the last to go home, and never, ever be both.
> *Anonymous*

1 GRAMMAR past simple: irregular verbs

a Change the sentences from the present to the past.

1 We meet in a café. (last night)
   We met in a café last night.
2 Max sees his friends after work. (last night)
   _____
3 Emily loses her keys. (yesterday)
   _____
4 We don't have dinner at home. (last night)
   _____
5 They leave work at 5.30. (yesterday)
   _____
6 Alex doesn't get up early. (yesterday morning)
   _____
7 My girlfriend feels ill. (yesterday)
   _____
8 Helen doesn't go out during the week. (last week)
   _____
9 I don't wear glasses. (yesterday)
   _____
10 Lucy can't come to my party. (last year)
   _____

b Complete the questions in the dialogue.

A	Where ¹ _did you go_ last night?
B	I went to that new sushi bar in town.
A	² _____ good?
B	Yes, it was great.
A	Who ³ _____ with?
B	I went with my girlfriend.
A	What ⁴ _____ ?
B	I wore jeans and my new black shirt.
A	What time ⁵ _____ home?
B	We got home at about midnight.
A	⁶ _____ a taxi home?
B	Yes. We didn't want to drive.
A	Did ⁷ _____ a good time?
B	Yes, we had a great time. The food was delicious!
A	⁸ _____ it expensive?
B	Yes, a bit.

2 VOCABULARY go, have, get

a ~~Cross out~~ the incorrect expression.

1 GO   to the beach   out   to a restaurant   ~~a bus~~
2 HAVE   lunch   a sandwich for a walk   a drink
3 GET   dressed   a good time up   an email
4 GO   to bed   a car   away   on holiday
5 HAVE   breakfast   a bike   a shower   18 years
6 GET   shopping   home   a newspaper   a taxi

b Complete the text with *went*, *had*, or *got*.

It was my girlfriend's birthday last Saturday, so we ¹ _went_ away for the weekend. I booked a hotel on the internet, and on Friday we ² _____ the train to the coast. It was quite late when we arrived, so we just ³ _____ a sandwich and ⁴ _____ to bed. The next day, we ⁵ _____ up early and ⁶ _____ breakfast in the hotel. It was a beautiful day, so we ⁷ _____ to the beach. We ⁸ _____ a swim in the morning, and in the afternoon we ⁹ _____ for a walk. In the evening, we ¹⁰ _____ dinner in an expensive French restaurant. The food was delicious! The next day was Sunday, so we ¹¹ _____ back home again. The weekend was very short, but we ¹² _____ a great time.

47

3 PRONUNCIATION irregular verbs, sentence stress

a Look at the pairs of irregular verbs. Do they have the same vowel sound? Write **S** (the same) or **D** (different).

1 came — had D
2 did — felt ☐
3 taught — wore ☐
4 could — spoke ☐
5 met — went ☐
6 knew — saw ☐
7 heard — left ☐
8 got — lost ☐

b **iChecker** Listen and check. Then listen and repeat the irregular verbs.

c **iChecker** Listen and repeat the sentences. Copy the rhythm.

> A What did you do last night?
> B I went to the cinema.
> A Who did you go with?
> B I went with a friend.
> A Where did you go after the film?
> B We went to a restaurant.
>   We didn't have an expensive meal.
>   We didn't get home late.

4 LISTENING

a **iChecker** Listen to an interview about a memorable night. What did Helen do?

b Listen again and answer the questions.

1 When was it?
2 Who was Helen with?
3 Where were they?
4 When did she arrive in the city?
5 Where did they have a drink?
6 Did they have a good time? Why (not)?
7 What did they have for dinner?
8 What time did they get home?

USEFUL WORDS AND PHRASES

Learn these words and phrases.

goal /ɡəʊl/
moon /muːn/
scarf /skɑːf/
screen /skriːn/
embarrassed /ɪmˈbærəst/
memorable /ˈmemərəbl/
decide /dɪˈsaɪd/
have a swim /hæv ə ˈswɪm/
know (somebody) a little /nəʊ ə ˈlɪtl/

iChecker TESTS FILE 7

Practical English Getting lost

1 VOCABULARY directions

Complete the words.

1 turn l_eft_
2 go str_____ o_____
3 turn r_____
4 go p_____ the station
5 on the c_____
6 o_____
7 a b_____
8 at the tr_____ l_____

2 ASKING FOR DIRECTIONS

Complete the dialogue with these words.

| exactly Excuse miss near say Sorry tell way Where's |

A ¹ _Excuse_ me, please. ² _____ the station?
B ³ _____, I don't live here.
A Excuse me. Is the station ⁴ _____ here?
C The station? It's near here, but I don't know ⁵ _____ where. Sorry.
A Excuse me. Can you ⁶ _____ me the ⁷ _____ to the station, please?
D Yes, of course. Go past the hotel, then turn left at the traffic lights. It's at the end of the street.
A Sorry, could you ⁸ _____ that again, please?
D Yes. Go past the hotel, then turn left at the traffic lights and it's at the end of the street. You can't ⁹ _____ it!
A Thank you.

3 SOCIAL ENGLISH

Complete the sentences with the words in the box.

| could course meet nice Maybe there What would |

1 _What_ a view!
2 What _____ you like to visit?
3 What is _____ to see?
4 We _____ go to the Houses of Parliament.
5 Would you like to _____ for lunch?
6 That's really _____ of you.
7 _____ another time.
8 Yes, of _____.

4 READING

a Read the information about getting around the UK.

Getting around the UK

By bus and coach
In the UK, long-distance express buses are called coaches. These are always economical, but they can be very slow. The biggest company is National Express, which has frequent services between big cities. They're usually cheaper if you buy your ticket early and travel at quiet times. In many towns, there are separate bus and coach stations, so passengers need to make sure they go to the right place to get their coach.

By car
Car travel in the UK is expensive, and there is often a lot of traffic. However, travelling by car means that you can be independent and flexible, and a car carrying three or more passengers can be cheaper than public transport. Motorways take drivers quickly from one city to the next, but small roads are often more scenic and fun. Parking in the centre of big cities can be difficult and very expensive, so an alternative is to use a Park & Ride. This is a system where drivers pay less to park their cars outside the city and take a bus to the centre.

By train
Trains are generally faster and more comfortable than coaches for long-distance travel, but they can be a lot more expensive. About 20 different companies operate train services in the UK, so the system can be quite confusing. However, passengers can get information on timetables and fares from the National Rail Enquiries website, which also has a way to buy tickets. There are two types of ticket: first and standard, and tickets are much cheaper if you buy them early.

b Read the information again. Write T (true) or F (false).

1 Taking a coach is a slow way to travel. _T_
2 The best time to travel by coach is at quiet times. __
3 There isn't much traffic in the UK. __
4 In a Park & Ride system you take a train. __
5 You can buy tickets from National Rail Enquiries. __

c Match the highlighted adjectives to their meanings.

1 beautiful _____
2 difficult to understand _____
3 quite cheap _____
4 normal _____
5 easy to change something _____
6 happening often _____

49

8A A murder story

Elementary, my dear Watson.
Attributed to Sherlock Holmes (but he never said it)

1 GRAMMAR past simple: regular and irregular

a Read this police report. Complete the sentences with the past simple form of the verbs brackets.

POLICE REPORT

Bank robbery

We ¹ _arrived_ (arrive) at the bank at 9.36 in the evening, and we ² _____ (park) our police car outside. The bank ³ _____ (be) closed and all the lights ⁴ _____ (be) off, but we ⁵ _____ (look) through the window. We ⁶ _____ (see) a person inside the bank. At first we ⁷ _____ (not can) see who it was, but then he ⁸ _____ (open) the door and came out – it was Steven Potter. He ⁹ _____ (not run) away – he just walked slowly to his car, and then drove away. The next morning, we ¹⁰ _____ (go) to his house at 6.00 a.m. We ¹¹ _____ (find) him in bed. He ¹² _____ (not want) to speak to us, but we ¹³ _____ (take) him to the police station.

b Complete the questions with the correct form of the verbs in brackets.

INSPECTOR	Where ¹ _were you_ at about 9.30 yesterday evening? (be)
STEVEN POTTER	I was at the cinema. The film ² _started_ at 9.00. (start)
I	What film ³ _____ ? (see)
SP	I can't remember. It wasn't very good.
I	Hmm. Very interesting. And who ⁴ _____ to the cinema with? (go)
SP	With my girlfriend.
I	⁵ _____ the film? (like)
SP	Yes, she thought it was very good.
I	What time ⁶ _____ the film _____ ? (finish)
SP	At about 10.30.
I	And what ⁷ _____ after you left the cinema? (do)
SP	We went to a restaurant – La Dolce Vita on the High Street.
I	La Dolce Vita? I know it. Very good spaghetti. What time ⁸ _____ the restaurant? (leave)
SP	At about 12.00.
I	That's very late. ⁹ _____ home after that? (go)
SP	No, we went to a nightclub – Flanagan's. Then we went home.
I	How? ¹⁰ _____ a taxi? (get)
SP	No, we got a bus.
I	And what time ¹¹ _____ to bed? (go)
SP	At about 4.00 a.m. Can I go home now? I'm tired.
I	No, I'd like to ask you some more questions…

50

2 VOCABULARY irregular verbs

a Complete the infinitive and past forms of these irregular verbs with *a, e, i, o,* or *u*.

Infinitive	Past
1 beg_i_n	beg_a_n
2 c__me	c__me
3 dr__nk	dr__nk
4 dr__ve	dr__ve
5 g__ve	g__ve
6 kn__w	kn__w
7 p__t	p__t
8 s__t	s__t
9 sw__m	sw__m
10 w__ke [up]	w__ke [up]
11 w__n	w__n
12 wr__te	wr__te

b Complete the sentences with the past simple form of the verbs in the box.

buy   find   break   ~~hear~~   make   take   can   lose   meet   think

1 Last night we _heard_ a noise downstairs.
2 They _____ the man's daughter was the murderer.
3 The policeman _____ the money in an old bag.
4 They _____ their friends outside the restaurant.
5 I _____ a detective story in the bookshop.
6 My girlfriend _____ her mobile phone last night.
7 The man _____ a window and went into the house.
8 Somebody _____ my laptop when I was out of the room.
9 We were worried because we _____ see a police car outside our house.
10 I was thirsty so I _____ a cup of tea.

3 PRONUNCIATION past simple verbs

a Match the verbs with the same vowel sound.

drove   could   ~~made~~   said   learnt   bought   had   lost

1 came   _made_
2 left   _____
3 got   _____
4 ran   _____
5 saw   _____
6 spoke   _____
7 took   _____
8 heard   _____

b **iChecker** Listen and check. Then listen and repeat.

4 LISTENING

a **iChecker** Listen to a radio interview with a detective. What does he like most about his job?
_____
_____

b **iChecker** Listen again and choose a, b, or c.
1 Jeremy Downs decided he wanted to be a detective…
   a when he was a child.
   b when he left school.
   c when he finished university.
2 His first job in the police was as…
   a an inspector.
   b a police officer.
   c a detective.
3 Jeremy took the … Exam to become a detective.
   a National Inspectors
   b National Detectives
   c National Investigators
4 Jeremy usually works…
   a outside.
   b in an office.
   c at the police station.
5 He sometimes feels…when he is at work.
   a bored
   b stressed
   c worried

USEFUL WORDS AND PHRASES

Learn these words and phrases.

library /ˈlaɪbri/
murder /ˈmɜːdə/
nobody /ˈnəʊbədi/
secretary /ˈsekrətri/
believe /bɪˈliːv/
kill /kɪl/
marry /ˈmæri/
business partner /ˈbɪznəs pɑːtnə/

If you want breakfast in bed, sleep in the kitchen.
Allison Pearson, British writer

8B A house with a history

1 GRAMMAR there is / there are, some / any + plural nouns

a Complete the dialogue with the correct form of *there is / there are* and, if necessary, *a*, *some*, or *any*.

A Hello. I'm interested in the flat to rent.
B Oh, OK Let me tell you about it. [1] _There's a_ large living room and [2] _____ small kitchen.
A [3] _____ table in the kitchen?
B No, [4] _____. But [5] _____ very nice dining room with a table and some chairs.
A That's fine. What about the bedrooms. How many bedrooms [6] _____?
B [7] _____ three bedrooms and a bathroom.
A [8] _____ shower in the bathroom?
B Yes, [9] _____.
A Good. [10] _____ bookshelves in the living room?
B No, I'm sorry. But [11] _____ cupboards.
A That's OK. I think it's perfect for us. How much is it?

b Write the sentences in the plural using *some* or *any*.

1 There's an armchair in the living room.
   There are some armchairs in the living room.
2 Is there a carpet downstairs?
   _____?
3 There's a CD on the shelf.
   _____.
4 Is there a glass in the cupboard?
   _____?
5 There isn't a file in the study.
   _____.

c Circle the correct form.

[1] **It's** / **There's** a nice flat and [2] **it isn't** / **there isn't** very expensive. [3] **There are** / **They are** two rooms but [4] **there aren't** / **they aren't** very big. [5] **There's** / **It is** a small kitchen and a bathroom. [6] **There isn't** / **It isn't** a bath in the bathroom, but [7] **it's** / **there's** a new shower. The flat is on the 10th floor, so [8] **there's** / **it is** a fantastic view of the city. And [9] **there's** / **it's** a very large balcony with a lot of flowers. [10] **They are** / **There are** beautiful in the summer!

2 VOCABULARY the house

a Complete the crossword.

52

b Write the room.
1 You usually take off your coat in the h_all_.
2 You usually have a shower in the b_____.
3 You usually have dinner in the d_____ r_____.
4 You usually use a computer in the st_____.
5 You usually park your car in the g_____.
6 You usually make lunch in the k_____.
7 You usually watch television in the l_____ r_____.
8 You usually sleep in the b_____.
9 You usually sit outside in the g_____.

3 PRONUNCIATION /ɪə/ and /eə/; word stress

a Circle the word with a different sound.

eə chair	1	they're	there	dear
ɪə ear	2	beer	stairs	near
eə chair	3	where	wear	we're
ɪə ear	4	here	hair	hear

b iChecker Listen and repeat the words.

c Underline the stressed syllable.
1 car|pet
2 mi|rror
3 cu|pboard
4 bal|co|ny
5 coo|ker
6 so|fa
7 arm|chair
8 ga|rage
9 cei|ling

d iChecker Listen and check. Then listen and repeat the words.

4 LISTENING

a iChecker Listen to Mrs Goodings show her house to Bradley and Joanna, a couple who are interested in renting it. Tick ✓ the **three** rooms Mrs Goodings shows them?
1 bathroom ☐
2 bedroom ☐
3 dining room ☐
4 garage ☐
5 hall ☐
6 kitchen ☐
7 living room ☐
8 study ☐

b iChecker Listen again and write T (true) or F (false).
1 Mrs Goodings always eats in the kitchen. _T_
2 Joanna doesn't like the living room. __
3 There isn't a washing machine in the kitchen. __
4 There's a hole in the ceiling of the kitchen. __
5 Joanna likes the windows in the living room. __
6 There isn't a TV in the living room. __
7 There are three bedrooms upstairs. __
8 Bradley forgets about the hole in the bathroom ceiling. __

USEFUL WORDS AND PHRASES

Learn these words and phrases.
advertisement /əd'vɜːtɪsmənt/
barman /'bɑːmən/
dishwasher /'dɪʃwɒʃə/
lovely /'lʌvli/
rent /rent/
a bottle of champagne /ə bɒtl ɒv ʃæm'peɪn/
a long time ago /ə lɒŋ taɪm ə'gəʊ/
(local) pub /pʌb/
Wow! /waʊ/
How horrible! /haʊ 'hɒrəbl/

> I'm not frightened of death.
> I just don't want to be there when it happens.
> Woody Allen, American film director

8C A night in a haunted hotel

1 GRAMMAR there was / there were

a Complete the text. Use *was*, *were*, *wasn't*, or *weren't*.

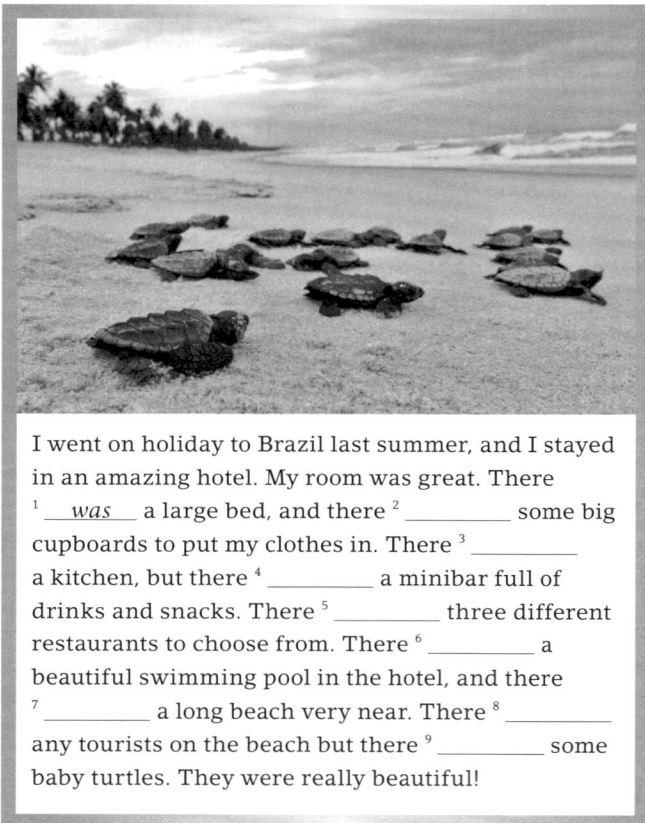

I went on holiday to Brazil last summer, and I stayed in an amazing hotel. My room was great. There ¹ _was_ a large bed, and there ² _____ some big cupboards to put my clothes in. There ³ _____ a kitchen, but there ⁴ _____ a minibar full of drinks and snacks. There ⁵ _____ three different restaurants to choose from. There ⁶ _____ a beautiful swimming pool in the hotel, and there ⁷ _____ a long beach very near. There ⁸ _____ any tourists on the beach but there ⁹ _____ some baby turtles. They were really beautiful!

b Complete the dialogue with a form of *there was / there were*.

A Did you have a good holiday?
B Not really. ¹ _There was_ a problem with my hotel.
A Oh dear. What happened?
B Well, we couldn't swim because ² _____ a swimming pool. And ³ _____ any restaurants near the hotel.
A ⁴ _____ a minibar in your room?
B No, ⁵ _____ a minibar and ⁶ _____ a television. The only thing in my room was the bed!
A Oh. ⁷ _____ a bathroom?
B Yes, but ⁸ _____ any clean towels. Everything was very dirty.
A ⁹ _____ any nice people in the hotel?
B Yes, ¹⁰ _____ some great people, but they all felt the same as me – very angry!

2 VOCABULARY prepositions: place and movement

Complete the sentences with these words.

| behind | from...to | in | in front of | next to | opposite |
| out of | over | under | up | | |

1 There's a family _in_ the dining room.
2 The boy is sitting _____ the girl.
3 The woman is _____ the man.
4 There's a ghost standing _____ the woman.
5 There's a bag _____ the table.
6 A waiter is coming _____ the kitchen.
7 There's a ghost _____ the waiter.
8 The waiter is carrying the plates _____ the kitchen _____ the tables.
9 There's a clock _____ the kitchen door.
10 A ghost is going _____ the stairs.

54

3 PRONUNCIATION silent letters

a Cross out the silent letters.
1 ghost   3 white   5 autumn   7 builder
2 cupboard   4 know   6 walk   8 wrong

b iChecker Listen and repeat. Copy the rhythm.

c iChecker Listen and underline the stressed words.
1 There was a lamp on the table.
2 There wasn't a bath in the bathroom.
3 Was there a mirror in the bedroom?
4 There were some books on the shelf.
5 There weren't any cupboards in the kitchen.
6 Were there any plants in the study?

d iChecker Listen again and repeat the sentences.

4 READING

Read the text. Write T (true) or F (false).
1 Maesmawr Hall is more than 500 years old.   _F_
2 People have seen ghosts inside and outside the hotel.   ___
3 The ghosts are all of people who lived in the house in the past.   ___
4 Robin Drwg's ghost sometimes appears as a bull.   ___
5 Paranormal investigators didn't think that Maesmawr Hall was haunted.   ___

5 LISTENING

a iChecker Listen to four people talking about hotel rooms. Which countries did they visit?

b Listen again. Match the speakers to the rooms.
Speaker 1 ☐   Speaker 2 ☐   Speaker 3 ☐   Speaker 4 ☐

A The room was under the water.
B The room had mirrors on the walls and the ceiling.
C The room wasn't very comfortable.
D The room was up a tree.

USEFUL WORDS AND PHRASES

Learn these words and phrases.

ghosts /gəʊsts/	haunted /ˈhɔːntɪd/
guest /gest/	strange /streɪndʒ/
owner /ˈəʊnə/	In the middle of the night
priest /priːst/	/ɪn ðə ˈmɪdl ɒv ðə ˈnaɪt/
brave /breɪv/	remote control /rɪməʊt kənˈtrəʊl/
frightened /ˈfraɪtnd/	

 FILE 8

Maesmawr Hall: A Haunted House in Wales

Maesmawr Hall is a manor house in Powys, Wales. It was built in 1535 and today is a 20-bedroom hotel and venue for weddings. It is famous because people say it is haunted.

Many guests say that they have seen ghosts. A businessman who stayed at the hotel said that when he looked out of the window he saw hundreds of Roman soldiers marching. In fact, in Roman times there was a road which passed through the grounds of Maesmawr Hall. Other guests said they saw the ghosts of the Davies sisters who owned the hotel in the 1900s, and the ghost of an old housekeeper walking through a wall in the hall. But perhaps most frightening is the story that the ghost of an evil man called Robin Drwg haunts the woods around the hotel. Some people say that they have seen this ghost suddenly change into the shape of a bull.

Maesmawr was on a TV programme about houses with ghosts called *Most Haunted*. The TV show presenters and investigators from the Mid Wales Paranormal (MWP) reported lots of strange activity in the hall – seeing balls of light, feeling movements, and hearing unusual sounds. During the investigation, the floor in one of the upstairs rooms moved. The hotel's current owner, Nigel Humphryson, says he often hears voices and banging noises that he cannot explain.

So if you're interested in ghosts, why not stay here? But don't go outside at night unless you're feeling really brave!

> To eat well in England, have breakfast three times a day.
> W Somerset Maugham, British writer

9A What I ate yesterday

1 GRAMMAR countable / uncountable nouns; a / an, some / any

a What did Sarah and Martin buy when they went shopping yesterday? Write *a*, *an*, or *some* in the gaps.

1 _some_ sausages
2 _____ lettuce
3 _____ eggs
4 _____ carrots
5 _____ jam
6 _____ orange
7 _____ pineapple
8 _____ crisps
9 _____ biscuits
10 _____ milk

b Write the sentences in the positive [+] or negative [–] form.

1 There's some ham in the fridge.
   [–] There _isn't any ham in the fridge_ .
2 There are some strawberries in our garden.
   [–] There _____ .
3 I didn't have an egg for breakfast.
   [+] I _____ .
4 There isn't any sugar in my tea.
   [+] There _____ .
5 I didn't eat any snacks yesterday.
   [+] I _____ .
6 There weren't any sandwiches in the kitchen.
   [+] There _____ .
7 I bought a pineapple at the supermarket.
   [–] I _____ .
8 There was some bread in the cupboard.
   [–] There _____ .

c Complete the dialogue with *a*, *an*, *some*, or *any*.

> **A** What do we need to buy for our dinner party? Let's make a list.
> **B** Well, I want to make [1] _a_ lasagne, so we need [2] _____ pasta and [3] _____ meat.
> **A** Pasta...and meat. What about tomatoes? Are there [4] _____ tomatoes in the fridge?
> **B** Let's have a look. There's [5] _____ onion, but there aren't [6] _____ tomatoes. Put those on the list, too.
> **A** Right...tomatoes. Is there [7] _____ cheese?
> **B** Yes, there's [8] _____ mozzarella cheese, so that's perfect.
> **A** Let's have [9] _____ salad with the lasagne.
> **B** OK. Then we need to buy [10] _____ lettuce.
> **A** What about dessert? Is there [11] _____ fruit?
> **B** No, there isn't. Let's get [12] _____ strawberries.

2 VOCABULARY food

a Complete the crossword.

b Write the words in the correct column.

apples   bananas   biscuits   carrots   chocolate   crisps
mushrooms   onions   oranges   peas   pineapple
potatoes   sandwiches   strawberries   sweets

Vegetables	Snacks	Fruit
_____	_____	_apples_
_____	_____	_____
_____	_____	_____
_____	_____	_____
_____	_____	_____

3 PRONUNCIATION the letters ea

a Circle the word with a different sound.

iː tree	1	m**ea**t br**ea**kfast t**ea**
e egg	2	br**ea**d h**ea**lthy ice cr**ea**m
eɪ train	3	**ea**t gr**ea**t st**ea**k

b **iChecker** Listen and check. Then listen and repeat the words.

4 READING

a Read the article and match the headings to the paragraphs.

| coconut water | ice lollies | roast camel |

b Read the article again. Write T (true) or F (false).

1 The Bedouin people eat roast camel on special occasions. T
2 There are seven ingredients in the Bedouin meal. __
3 Frank Epperson's drink froze because the weather was cold. __
4 He sold his first ice lolly when he was 29 years old. __
5 According to the article, you can find coconut water in all coconuts. __
6 Coconut water has a lot of sugar. __

c Guess the meaning of the highlighted words. Check in your dictionary.

5 LISTENING

a **iChecker** Listen to four speakers talking about their favourite meal. Complete the meals.

Speaker 1 roast _____
Speaker 2 _____ tikka masala
Speaker 3 _____ and chips
Speaker 4 sweet and sour _____

b **iChecker** Listen again. Match the speakers to the sentences.

Speaker 1 ☐ A I often eat it outside.
Speaker 2 ☐ B I always order rice with it.
Speaker 3 ☐ C I have it at a local restaurant.
Speaker 4 ☐ D I eat it when I visit my parents.

USEFUL WORDS AND PHRASES

Learn these words and phrases.

cream /kriːm/
dishes /ˈdɪʃɪz/
ingredients /ɪnˈɡriːdiənts/
popcorn /ˈpɒpkɔːn/
sauce /sɔːs/
sweetcorn /ˈswiːtkɔːn/
takeaway (food) /ˈteɪkəweɪ/
delicious /dɪˈlɪʃəs/
vegetarian /vedʒəˈteəriən/
a glass (of wine) /ə ɡlɑːs/

Three interesting food facts

1 _____

The Bedouin people, who live in the deserts of Africa, sometimes prepare a very big meal to celebrate weddings. The cook uses some eggs, some fish, some chickens, a sheep, and a camel to prepare it. He stuffs the fish with the eggs, the chickens with the fish, the sheep with the chickens, and the camel with the sheep. Then he cooks all the ingredients together in an enormous oven in the ground.

2 _____

It was an 11-year-old American boy who invented these. In 1905, the boy, Frank Epperson, wanted to make a drink. He put some soda powder in a cup of water and used a stick to mix it. Then he forgot about the drink and left it outside. That night it was very cold, so the mixture froze. Eighteen years later, he made some more of the frozen mixture and sold his first one at an amusement park. Americans call them 'popsicles'.

3 _____

You can find this liquid in young fruit that are still green. People drank it in South-East Asia, Africa, and the Caribbean before it became popular as a health drink. Today athletes drink it after doing sport. It is very good for you as it is low in fats and sugars. Doctors sometimes use it in an emergency because it is similar to human plasma.

57

Human beings are 70% water.
With some people, the rest is collagen.
Martin Mull, American actor and writer

9B White gold

1 GRAMMAR quantifiers: *how much / how many, a lot of*, etc.

a Complete the questions. Then complete the sentences.

How much salt do you have with your meals?

Not much.

1 He *doesn't have much salt with his meals*.

_____ _____ sugar do you put in your tea?

A lot.

2 He _____.

_____ _____ biscuits do you eat?

Not many.

3 She _____.

_____ sweets do you buy?

Quite a lot.

4 He _____.

_____ exercise do you do?

Not much.

5 He _____.

_____ _____ cups of coffee do you drink?

None.

6 She _____.

b Read the information and write questions.

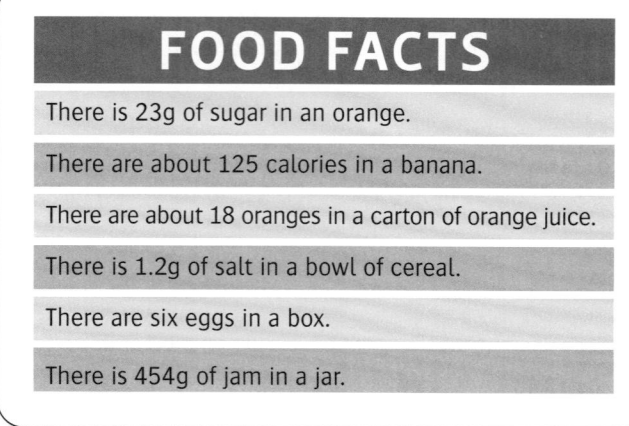

FOOD FACTS
There is 23g of sugar in an orange.
There are about 125 calories in a banana.
There are about 18 oranges in a carton of orange juice.
There is 1.2g of salt in a bowl of cereal.
There are six eggs in a box.
There is 454g of jam in a jar.

1 _How much sugar is there in an orange_ ?
Answer: 23g.
2 _____?
Answer: About 125.
3 _____?
Answer: About 18.
4 _____?
Answer: 1.2g.
5 _____?
Answer: six.
6 _____?
Answer: 454g.

58

2 VOCABULARY food containers

a Unscramble the words to make food containers.
1 rja — *jar*
2 bxo — _____
3 rncoat — _____
4 nit — _____
5 cpeatk — _____
6 nca — _____
7 totble — _____

b Complete the sentences with a container from **a**.
1 She was thirsty, so she bought a __can__ of fizzy drink.
2 Do you need the scissors to open the _____ of juice?
3 He took the _____ of strawberry jam out of the cupboard.
4 There is a small _____ of crisps in that big bag.
5 We always take a _____ of water when we go for a walk.
6 They made some sandwiches with a _____ of tuna.
7 I gave her a _____ of chocolates to say thank you.

3 PRONUNCIATION /ʃ/ and /s/

a Circle the word with a different sound.

snake	1	**s**ugar	**s**alad	**c**ereal
shower	2	**s**ure	fre**sh**	**s**alt
snake	3	ri**c**e	**sh**opping	**sc**ience
shower	4	**sh**ort	informa**ti**on	**ce**ntre

b iChecker Listen and check. Then listen and repeat the words.

c iChecker Listen and repeat the sentences.
1 She saw Susan standing outside the cinema.
2 Shawn said sorry for singing in the shower.
3 Steve puts six spoons of sugar on his cereal.
4 Sylvia spends Saturdays in the shopping centre.

4 LISTENING

a iChecker Listen to the radio show about food groups. Complete the examples of the groups.

1 carbohydrates: bread, pasta, _____, potatoes
2 fruits and vegetables: apples, oranges, _____, carrots
3 protein: meat, _____
4 milk and dairy: _____, yoghurt
5 fats and sugars: cakes, _____, sweets, crisps

b iChecker Listen again. Complete the gaps with one word.
1 Carbohydrates give us _____.
2 Fruits and vegetables contain important _____.
3 Protein helps our bodies to _____ and repair.
4 Milk and dairy are important for our bones and _____.
5 You should eat fats and sugars _____ or _____ a week.

USEFUL WORDS AND PHRASES

Learn these words and phrases.

gold /gəʊld/
spoon /spuːn/
vitamins /ˈvɪtəmɪnz/
fresh /freʃ/
spoonful /ˈspuːnfʊl/
instead of /ɪnˈsted əv/

9C Quiz night

Imagination is more important than knowledge.
Albert Einstein, German scientist

1 GRAMMAR comparative adjectives

a Write the comparative forms of these adjectives in the correct circle.

| bad beautiful cheap dry sad difficult dirty |
| cold far wet high hungry comfortable thin good |

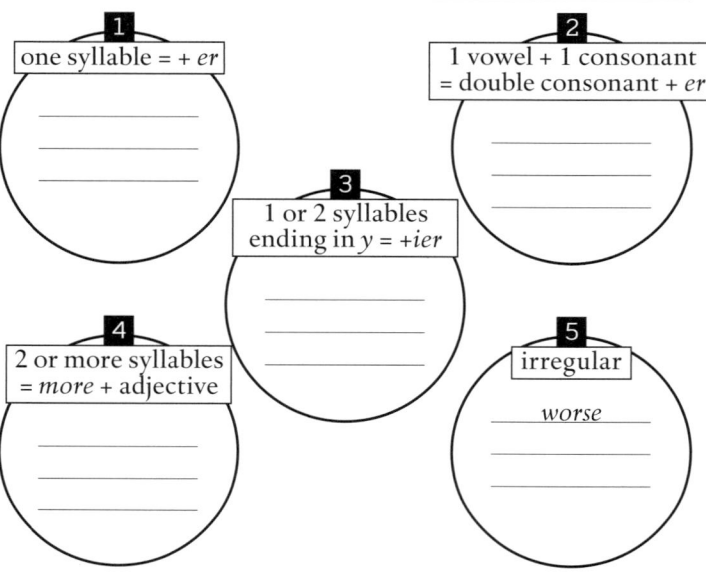

b Write sentences using the opposite adjective.
1 A bike is slower than a car.
   A car _is faster than a bike_.
2 Lions are smaller than tigers.
   Tigers _____.
3 Ireland is wetter than Italy.
   Italy _____.
4 January is longer than February.
   February _____.
5 A laptop is more expensive than an iPod.
   An iPod _____.
6 Fridays are better than Mondays.
   Mondays _____.
7 A cooker is hotter than a fridge.
   A fridge _____.
8 Italian is easier than Russian.
   Russian _____.

2 VOCABULARY high numbers

a **iChecker** Listen and circle the correct numbers.
1 104   304
2 586   596
3 2,670   2,660
4 8,905   9,905
5 11,750   12,750
6 543,830   553,830
7 1,315,000   1,350,000
8 25,460,000   35,460,000

b **iChecker** Listen and write the numbers in words.
1 125 _____
2 895 _____
3 4,500 _____
4 12,470 _____
5 33,930 _____
6 575,600 _____
7 6,250,000 _____
8 34,800,265 _____

3 PRONUNCIATION /ə/, sentence stress

a Write the words in the chart.

| better cheaper colder dirtier drier easier |
| healthier higher shorter slower taller worse |

iː tree	ɔː horse	ɜː bird	e egg	əʊ phone	aɪ bike
___	___	___	_better_	___	___

b **iChecker** Listen and repeat.

60

c **iChecker** Listen and underline the stressed words.
1 A pencil is cheaper than a pen.
2 June is shorter than July.
3 The kitchen is dirtier than the living room.
4 An apple is healthier than a biscuit.
5 Switzerland is colder than France.
6 Everest is higher than Kilimanjaro.

d **iChecker** Listen again and repeat the sentences. Copy the rhythm.

4 READING

a Read the sentences. Do you think they are T (true) or F (false)? Then read the article and check.
1 Cycling is safer than driving. ___
2 Dogs are more intelligent than cats. ___
3 South America is bigger than North America. ___
4 Margarine is healthier than butter. ___

b Guess the meaning of the highlighted words. Check the meaning and pronunciation in your dictionary.

5 LISTENING

iChecker Listen to a conversation between a couple talking about two cities with the same name. Write T (true) or F (false).
1 More people live in Birmingham UK than Birmingham USA. T
2 Birmingham UK is bigger than Birmingham USA. ___
3 Birmingham USA is greener than Birmingham UK. ___
4 Birmingham USA is older than Birmingham UK. ___
5 Birmingham USA is wetter than Birmingham UK. ___
6 Birmingham UK is colder than Birmingham USA. ___

USEFUL WORDS AND PHRASES

Learn these words and phrases.

contestants /kənˈtestənts/
population /ˌpɒpjuˈleɪʃn/
prize /praɪz/
approximately /əˈprɒksɪmətli/
win a competition /wɪn ə kɒmpəˈtɪʃn/

 FILE 9

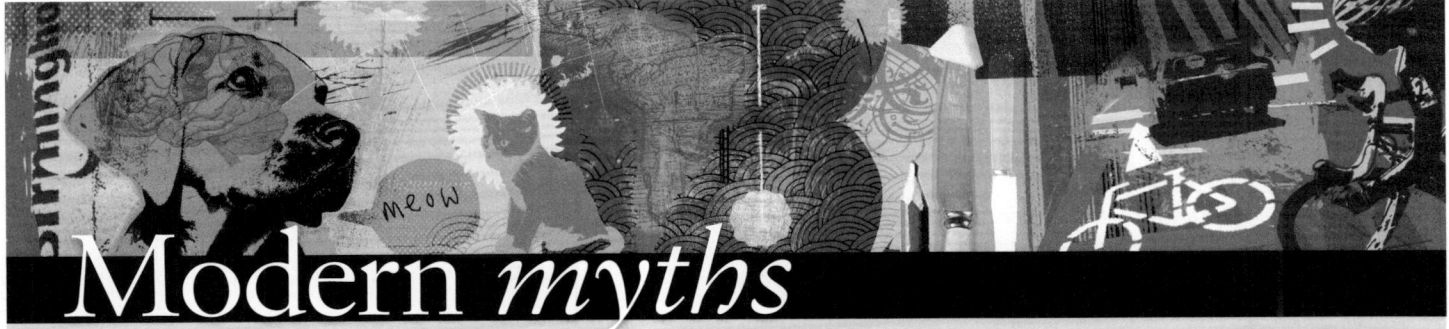

Modern *myths*

1 Scientists at Oxford University did some research into the brains of different groups of mammals . They looked at the changes in the size of the brains over the last 60 million years and they discovered that there were bigger changes in dogs' brains than there were in cats' brains. They think that dogs are cleverer than cats because they are more social.

2 There are 12 countries in South America including Argentina and Brazil. It has an area of 17,840,000 square kilometres and its population is over 371,090,000. North America includes Canada and the USA but it also contains the countries of Central America. It covers an area of about 24,709,000 square kilometres and its population is nearly 529 million. This makes it bigger than South America.

3 When the British Medical Journal studied the number of people injured in traffic accidents in the UK, they got a surprise. They discovered that for every 100 car passengers who went to hospital, there were 68 cyclists. However, a lot of people travel by car, and only a few go by bike, so the results show that cycling is actually more dangerous than driving.

4 Experts have different opinions about margarine and butter, and there is a big argument about which one is better for you. The truth is that margarine today is better than it was in the past because producers use a different type of vegetable oil. Butter still contains a lot of animal fat. Margarine today contains less fat which makes it healthier than butter.

61

Practical English At a restaurant

1 VOCABULARY AND READING

a Look at the menu and answer the questions.

1 Which is the best starter for somebody on a diet?
2 What main course can a vegetarian have?
3 Can you have fruit for dessert?
4 How many types of coffee are there?
5 Do children pay the same as adults?

Taste of Heaven Restaurant
MENU

Starters
Chicken soup	£3.50
Prawn cocktail	£4.25
Grilled vegetables with low-fat cheese (V)	£4.75

Salads
Mixed salad (V)	£5.50
Seafood salad	£7.25

Main courses
Roast beef served with roast potatoes and vegetables	£12.25
Mushroom risotto with Parmesan cheese (V)	£9.50
Fried salmon served with chips and peas	£10.75

Desserts
Fresh fruit salad	£3.95
Chocolate brownie with cream	£4.50
New York cheesecake	£4.25

Beverages
Glass of wine (red or white)	£2.95
Bottle of wine (red or white)	£10.50
Beer	£3.50
Soft drinks	£2.75
Coffee (espresso or latte)	£2.25

Set menu
£14.95 (see the board for today's choice)

25% discount on children's portions
(V) Suitable for vegetarians

b Underline the words or phrases you don't know. Use your dictionary to look up their meaning and pronunciation.

2 ORDERING A MEAL

Complete the dialogue with <u>one</u> word in each gap.

A Good evening. Do you have a [1] _reservation_ ?
B Yes, a [2] _____ for two. My name's Miriam Kieslowski.
A Come this [3] _____, please.
A Are you ready to [4] _____?
B Yes. The grilled vegetables and the mushroom risotto, please.
C [5] _____ like the prawn cocktail and then the roast beef, please.
A What would you [6] _____ to drink?
C [7] _____ water for me.
B A bottle of mineral water, please.
A [8] _____ or sparkling?
B Is sparkling OK?
C Yes, sparkling.
A Thank you, madam.
B Thank you.

3 SOCIAL ENGLISH

Match the sentences 1–6 to the correct responses a–f.

1 What do you do on your birthday? [c]
2 Would you like a dessert? [ ]
3 A decaf espresso. [ ]
4 Can I use your phone? [ ]
5 Good news? [ ]
6 Could we have the bill, please? [ ]

a Not for me, thanks.
b Yes. I got the job!
c ~~Nothing special.~~
d Yes, of course, sir.
e The same for me, please.
f Yes, go ahead.

10A The most dangerous road...

> As soon as there is life there is danger.
> Ralph Waldo Emerson, American writer

1 GRAMMAR superlative adjectives

a Complete the chart.

Adjective	Comparative	Superlative
1 cold	*colder*	*the coldest*
2 high		
3 expensive		
4 dry		
5 dangerous		
6 hot		
7 beautiful		
8 interesting		
9 good		
10 bad		

b Write the questions.

1 What / small continent / world
  What's the smallest continent in the world ?
2 What / big ocean / world
  _____ ?
3 What / large country / world
  _____ ?
4 What / populated city / world
  _____ ?
5 What / wet place / world
  _____ ?
6 What / dry desert / world
  _____ ?
7 What / common native language / world
  _____ ?
8 What / cold place / world
  _____ ?

c Circle the correct answer to the questions in **b**.

1 a (Australia)
  b Europe
  c South America
2 a The Atlantic
  b The Pacific
  c The Indian Ocean
3 a Canada
  b China
  c Russia
4 a Mumbai
  b Shanghai
  c Buenos Aires
5 a India
  b Ireland
  c Brazil
6 a The Sahara Desert (Africa)
  b The Arizona Desert (The USA)
  c The Atacama Desert (South America)
7 a Mandarin Chinese
  b English
  c Hindi
8 a The Arctic
  b Alaska
  c The Antarctic

2 VOCABULARY places and buildings

a Complete the sentences with a word in each box.

art car department police post railway ~~shopping~~ town

~~centre~~ gallery hall office park station station store

1 Where can you visit different shops?
  At a __*shopping centre*__.
2 Where can you see paintings?
  In an _____ _____.
3 Where can you get a train from?
  From a _____ _____.
4 Where can you buy a stamp?
  At a _____ _____.
5 Where can you talk to a policeman?
  At a _____ _____.
6 Where can you buy clothes for all the family?
  In a _____ _____.
7 Where can you leave your car?
  At a _____ _____.
8 Where can you speak to a local politician?
  In the _____ _____.

63

b Complete the puzzle. Can you find the hidden word?

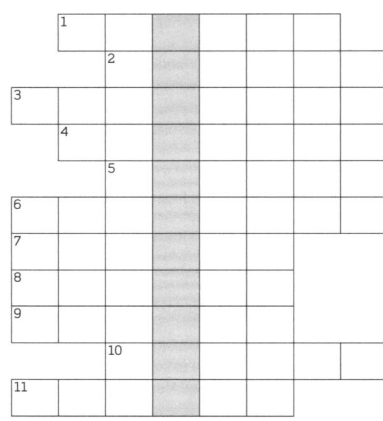

3 PRONUNCIATION consonant groups

iChecker Listen and repeat the sentences.

1. It's the cheapest place to live.
2. It's the highest mountain in the world.
3. He's the healthiest person in the family.
4. It's the prettiest village in the country.
5. It's the most difficult language to learn.
6. It's the most polluted city in the area.
7. They're the most attractive couple I know.
8. She's the most intelligent person in the class.

4 LISTENING

a **iChecker** Listen to a radio interview with a travel writer. What is his book called? _____

b **iChecker** Listen again. Complete the sentences.

1. Uluru is the _____ rock in the world.
2. It's _____ kilometres long.
3. The world's highest waterfall is in _____.
4. The tallest building in the world is _____ metres high.
5. The world's oldest city began in _____ BC.
6. The world's longest railway goes from _____ to Vladivostok.
7. The shortest runway in the world is _____ metres long.

5 READING

a Read the text and write T (true) or F (false).

1. Ulm Münster is the world's biggest church. ___
2. You can sometimes see the mountains from the top of the church. ___
3. Ulm Münster was the city's first church. ___
4. Construction of the church took over 500 years. ___
5. The church opens every day at 8 o'clock. ___
6. It's very expensive to visit Ulm Münster. ___

b Guess the meaning of the highlighted words. Check in your dictionary.

THE SKY'S THE LIMIT

Ulm Münster in Germany is the tallest church in the world. The tallest part of the church is the steeple, which is 161.5 metres high and contains 768 steps. From the top of the church there is a view of the city, and on a clear day you can see the Alps.

Before the Münster was built, Ulm already had a church outside the city walls. However, the inhabitants of the city decided that they wanted a new church in the town centre and they agreed to pay for the building.

Construction of the church began in 1377 but the building wasn't completed until 31st May, 1890. At first the work was difficult because the heaviest parts fell down and the builders had to repair them. Then construction stopped from 1543 to 1817 for political reasons.

Today, tourists can visit the church every day of the year. Winter opening hours are from 9 a.m. to 4.45 p.m. and the church is open in the summer months from 8 a.m. to 7.45 p.m. Admission to the church is free, but the price of climbing the steeple is €3 for adults and €2 for children.

USEFUL WORDS AND PHRASES

Learn these words and phrases.

accidents /ˈæksɪdənts/
fun /fʌn/
region /ˈriːdʒən/
nearly /ˈnɪəli/
popular /ˈpɒpjələ/
wide (*opposite* narrow) /waɪd/
below (*opposite* above) /bɪˈləʊ/

To travel hopefully is a better thing than to arrive.
Robert Louis Stevenson, Scottish writer

10B CouchSurf round the world!

1 GRAMMAR be going to (plans), future time expressions

a Order the words to make sentences.

1 are / there / you / get / to / How / going
   How are you going to get there?
2 to / isn't / He / a / going / stay / in / hotel
   _____.
3 show / to / They're / city / going / the / me
   _____.
4 good / going / time / have / We're / to / a
   _____.
5 is / home / to / she / going / When / go
   _____?
6 not / sights / going / I'm / see / the / to
   _____.

b Complete the sentences. Use the correct form of *going to*.

1 _Are they going to leave_ by train? (they / leave)
2 We _____ our friends the city. (show)
3 They _____ nice meals in expensive restaurants. (have)
4 _____ with a friend? (you / stay)
5 They _____ the museum. (not visit)
6 _____ the sights? (they / see)
7 He _____ a lot of people. (meet)
8 She _____ on holiday this year. (not go)

c Complete the dialogue. Use the correct form of *going to*.

A So, where ¹ _are you going to go_ (go) on holiday?
B I ² _____ (travel) round Europe for a few weeks.
A Really? Where ³ _____ (stay)?
B Well, this year I ⁴ _____ (not/sleep) in hotels. Instead, I'm going to CouchSurf.
A CouchSurf? What a great idea! ⁵ _____ (travel) alone?
B Yes, I am. My girlfriend ⁶ _____ (drive) to Marbella with some friends. They ⁷ _____ (spend) all day on the beach and they ⁸ _____ (dance) all night. I don't like that kind of holiday. I ⁹ _____ (meet) lots of new people and see lots of new places.
A Which countries ¹⁰ _____ ? (visit)
B Italy first, and then Croatia, Greece, and Turkey. My CouchSurfing hosts ¹¹ _____ (show) me the sights. I ¹² _____ (have) a great time!

2 VOCABULARY holidays

a Write the expressions in the correct column.

~~back home~~   by train   a good time   on holiday
the sights   in a hotel   nice meals
somebody around your town   with a friend

GO	back home
HAVE	
SEE	
SHOW	
STAY	

b Complete the text with the verbs from **a**.

Maria is really happy because she's going to ¹ _go_ on holiday tomorrow. She's going to ² _____ with her cousins in London. They're going to ³ _____ her around the city and she's going to ⁴ _____ all the sights. They're going to ⁵ _____ lots of nice meals together. She's going to ⁶ _____ by plane, and she's going to ⁷ _____ in London for a week. The second week, Maria and her cousins are going to travel to the coast. They're going to ⁸ _____ in a hotel, and they're going to ⁹ _____ a great time. Maria's going to ¹⁰ _____ back to London before she goes home.

65

3 PRONUNCIATION sentence stress

a **iChecker** Listen and underline the stressed words.
1 How are you going to get there?
2 Where are you going to stay?
3 We're going to stay for a week.
4 I'm going to see the sights.
5 We aren't going to go by car.
6 I'm not going to stay in a hotel.

b **iChecker** Listen again and repeat the sentences. Copy the rhythm.

4 LISTENING

a **iChecker** Listen to four speakers talking about their first experience of CouchSurfing. How many people did not enjoy the experience? _____

b **iChecker** Listen again and match the speakers to the sentences A–D.

Speaker 1 ☐   Speaker 3 ☐
Speaker 2 ☐   Speaker 4 ☐

A CouchSurfing gave me the chance to make friends.
B CouchSurfing helped me with my work.
C My host was also my tourist guide to the city.
D My second experience of CouchSurfing was better than the first.

5 READING

a Read the text. Answer the questions with **H** (Hannah), **A** (Arno), **V** (Virginie), or **R** (Rory).
1 Which person made new friends while travelling? ☐
2 Who spent very little on accommodation? ☐
3 Who used their InterRail pass on another form of transport? ☐
4 Who was travelling abroad for the first time? ☐
5 Which person found it easy to make new plans while travelling? ☐

USEFUL WORDS AND PHRASES

Learn these words and phrases.

couch /kaʊtʃ/
flatmate /ˈflætmeɪt/
a host /ə ˈhəʊst/
tap /tæp/
create a profile /kriˈeɪt ə ˈprəʊfaɪl/
recommend (things to do) /rekəˈmend/
Have a good trip! /əv ə ɡʊd ˈtrɪp/
It's free. /ɪts ˈfriː/

Travelling by InterRail

Since 1972, backpackers have enjoyed the freedom to explore 30 European countries, thanks to the InterRail pass. Here, InterRail travellers say why they love InterRail so much.

Hannah Kopper (23, England)

Route
Amsterdam – Hamburg – Berlin – Warsaw – Krakow – Prague – Vienna – Budapest – Zagreb – Split – Mostar – Sarajevo – Belgrade

I love InterRail because you can go where you want, when you want! When we started our journey, we had an idea of where we wanted to go, but as we travelled we got new ideas. Changing our plans was easy – you can stay an extra night or two if you like a place, and if you don't like it you can go somewhere else. The InterRail pass gives you real freedom.

Arno Valentjin (29, The Netherlands)

Route
Amsterdam – Bonn – Stuttgart – Salzburg – Ljubljana – Split – Pescara – Bari – Corfu – Igoumenitsa – Patras – Athens

One of the best things about InterRail is that you get cheaper, or even free travel on ferries as well as trains. I travelled to Split in Croatia and then took the ferry to Pescara in Italy. Then I travelled by InterRail to the south of Italy, and then took the ferry to the Greek island of Corfu. It was fantastic! You also get discounts on hotels, tourist attractions, and lots more.

Virginie Gauguet (26, France)

Route
Paris – Versailles – Épernay – Blois – Angers – Lyons – Chamonix – Nice – Monaco – Ventimiglia – Pisa – Florence – Perugia – Assisi – Rome – Naples

In six weeks I met so many new interesting people and made friends from all over the world. It's a cheap way to travel too, especially if you take the night trains – I saved a lot of money on accommodation this way. I really want to go InterRailing again!

Rory Mitchell (21, Scotland)

Route
Innsbruck – Venice – Sienna – Lucca – Pisa – Florence – Cannes – Monaco – Nice – Figueras – Rosas – Barcelona – Paris – Antwerp

This was the first time I'd left the UK, and I loved it. InterRail is safe and easy for first-time travellers. I got an InterRail Global Pass so I could take as many trains as I wanted. I saw many amazing places, and learnt a lot about Europe's culture and history. I visited over 15 cities in less than a month. I'm definitely going to do it again next year!

> Love cannot save you from your own fate.
> Jim Morrison, singer with The Doors

10C What's going to happen?

1 GRAMMAR *be going to* (predictions)

a Look at the pictures. Write sentences using these verbs and *be going to*.

buy change ~~eat~~ have listen lose read take

1 _They're going to eat_ a pizza.
2 _____ some money.
3 _____ a newspaper.
4 _____ a coffee.
5 _____ to music.
6 _____ a book.
7 _____ a photo.
8 _____ his passport.

b Write a letter in the box: **A** = plan, **B** = prediction.

1 I'm going to buy some stamps. _A_
2 It's going to be cold tomorrow. ☐
3 Jim's going to study tonight. ☐
4 Our team is going to lose this match. ☐
5 There's going to be a storm later. ☐
6 I think that restaurant's going to close. ☐
7 They're going to buy a new TV. ☐
8 I'm going to book a flight online. ☐

2 VOCABULARY verb phrases

Complete the phrases with verbs from the box.

~~be~~ become fall get (x3) ~~have~~ meet move travel

1 _be_ lucky
2 _____ somebody new
3 _____ to a different country
4 _____ married
5 _have_ a lot of money
6 _____ in love
7 _____ famous
8 _____ a new job
9 _____ a surprise
10 _____ house

3 PRONUNCIATION the letters oo

a Look at the pairs of words. Tick ✓ the pairs with the same sound and cross ✗ the pairs that are different.

1	choose	school	✓
2	book	soon	✗
3	food	moon	
4	good	cook	
5	took	spoon	
6	look	too	

b **iChecker** Listen and check. Then listen and repeat.

4 READING

a Read the text. Match the headings to the paragraphs.
  1 Give me your hand
  2 Let's play cards
  3 How do you like your tea?
  4 What's inside the ball?

b Read the text again and write T (true) or F (false).
  1 The easiest way to read Tarot cards is to use four cards. ___
  2 An image of a nurse means bad health. ___
  3 A strong Heart line means you're going to find love. ___
  4 A shape of a bird means bad luck. ___

c Guess the meaning of the highlighted words. Check in your dictionary.

5 LISTENING

a **iChecker** Listen to Pete and Amy's conversation about the psychic Uri Geller. Was his trick with the spoons real?
___

b **iChecker** Listen again and write T (true) or F (false).
  1 A lot of people watched Uri Geller in the past. ___
  2 Pete and Amy see a video of the trick. ___
  3 Amy doesn't believe the trick at first. ___
  4 Uri doesn't use a normal spoon. ___
  5 Uri doesn't speak during the trick. ___
  6 Today, Uri doesn't appear in public. ___

The name behind the method

A ___

In tasseography, the fortune-teller uses tea leaves to predict the future. You drink a cup of tea and leave a small amount in the bottom of the cup. Then you move the tea round the cup three times, cover it with a saucer, and turn it upside down. The fortune-teller looks at the shape the tea leaves make. For example, a bird means that you're going to have good news.

B ___

In crystallomancy, the fortune-teller uses a glass ball. She places the ball on the table between you and her, and looks into it for a long period of time. At first, the ball looks dull and cloudy, but then it clears and images start to appear. The fortune-teller uses these pictures to predict your future. For example, a nurse means that you're going to be ill.

C ___

In Tarot reading, the fortune-teller uses a special pack of Tarot cards to predict the future. There are 78 cards in the pack, and there are different ways of using them. The quickest is to lay three cards on the table from left to right. The cards represent the past, the present, and the future. The fortune-teller turns over the cards and says what they mean. For example, the Sun means that you're going to become famous.

D ___

Chiromancy is also called palmistry and it's when the fortune-teller studies the lines on the palm of your hand to predict your future. There are four major lines on the hand: the Life line, the Head line, the Heart line, and the Health line. For example, a strong Heart line means that you're going to find the right partner and be happy in your life.

USEFUL WORDS AND PHRASES

Learn these words and phrases.

soon /suːn/
be lucky /bi ˈlʌki/
Come in! /kʌm ɪn/
get married /get ˈmærid/
move to another country /muːv tu əˈnʌðə ˈkʌntri/

iChecker TESTS FILE 10

11A First impressions

> You can fall in love at first sight with a place as with a person.
> Alec Waugh, British writer

1 GRAMMAR adverbs (manners and modifiers)

a Complete the sentences with an adverb.

1 The French cook perfect meals.
  They cook __perfectly__.
2 The Germans are careful drivers.
  They drive _____.
3 The British are very polite.
  They speak very _____.
4 The Brazilians are good at football.
  They play football _____.
5 The Japanese are very hard workers.
  They work very _____.
6 The Canadians eat healthy food.
  They eat _____.
7 The Swedish speak beautiful English.
  They speak English _____.

b Circle the correct word.

1 My brother dresses **casual** / **casually**.
2 Frank cooks **real** / **really** well.
3 It's **easy** / **easily** to ride a bike.
4 They walked **quick** / **quickly** to the railway station.
5 He's very **quiet** / **quietly**. He never says anything!
6 Elena's pizzas are **incredible** / **incredibly**.
7 My French is very **bad** / **badly**.
8 Can you speak more **slow** / **slowly**?
9 Mark speaks English **good** / **well**.
10 She eats **unhealthily** / **unhealthy**.
11 They have **real** / **really** stressful jobs.

2 VOCABULARY common adverbs

Make adverbs from the adjectives and complete the sentences.

careful good easy hard healthy incredible perfect quiet

In the ideal city...
1 ...car drivers drive __carefully__.
2 ...workers work _____.
3 ...families eat _____.
4 ...people speak foreign languages _____.
5 ...you can travel around _____.
6 ...people talk _____.
7 ...everybody treats tourists _____.
8 ...everything is _____ cheap.

3 PRONUNCIATION word stress

a Underline the stressed syllable in the adverbs. Which **three** adverbs are not stressed on the first syllable?

_____, _____, _____

1 beau|ti|fu|lly   6 in|cre|di|bly
2 care|fu|lly   7 per|fect|ly
3 ca|sua|lly   8 po|lite|ly
4 dan|ge|rous|ly   9 un|heal|thi|ly
5 fash|ion|ably

b iChecker Listen and check. Then listen and repeat the adverbs.

69

4 READING

a Read the text. Match the headings A–D to the paragraphs.

A The Polish way of life
B Feeling at home abroad
C My first impressions
D Not what I expected

First impressions of Warsaw

Danny MacIntyre, from Scotland, came to Poland for the first time seven years ago. He now lives in Warsaw where he runs a small media company.

1 _____

You always remember your first impressions of a new country. When I first came to Warsaw, I didn't know much about Poland at all. I didn't know anything about the culture. I didn't think the food was going to be very exciting, and I expected the weather to be similar to Scotland – maybe even a bit colder! But when I got there, I discovered how wrong I was.

2 _____

It was summer, and it was hot! In fact, the temperature was over 30 degrees! My first impression was that Warsaw was more beautiful than I expected. I spent a lot of time just walking around looking at the incredible architecture. I felt that the city had wonderful atmosphere and lots of energy.

3 _____

Polish people are very friendly. Most people can speak a bit of English and many speak it very well. I am trying to learn Polish, but it is very difficult. Fortunately, people don't mind when I make mistakes! Polish people are very hospitable, and they love to socialize – get together, eat, drink, and talk. Parties often don't finish until early the next morning. I am now married to a Polish woman. At our wedding, our guests didn't leave until 5.00 a.m. the next morning!

4 _____

Poland is a great place to live. It has everything – friendly people; cheap travel; delicious food; the summers are hot; and there's great skiing in the winter. There are mountains, lakes, and beaches; beautiful cities and fascinating culture. I still love Scotland, but Poland feels like home now.

b Complete the sentences with words in the box.

atmosphere culture socializing fascinating hospitality
impressions architecture expect

1 Danny's first _____ of Warsaw are very memorable.
2 Before he got to Poland, Danny didn't know much about Polish _____.
3 He didn't _____ the city to be so beautiful.
4 He was very impressed by the _____ in Warsaw.
5 He also liked the energy and _____ of the city.
6 The _____ of the Polish people is well known.
7 Polish people like _____ with their family and friends.
8 Danny finds the Polish culture _____.

5 LISTENING

iChecker Listen to two people talking about where they live. Answer the questions.

Speaker 1   Brno, Czech Republic

1 Why is the city so quiet and empty at the weekend?
2 Where are there lots of shops?
3 How are they different from the ones in the main shopping areas?

Speaker 2   Reykjavik, Iceland

4 When do people go to swimming pools and hot tubs?
5 What are there very few of in the Icelandic countryside?
6 How many people are there…?
   in Reykjavik
   in the second-biggest city
7 What kind of things do Icelandic people make?

USEFUL WORDS AND PHRASES

Learn these words and phrases.

a foreigner   /ə ˈfɒrənə/
myth   /mɪθ/
subtitles   /ˈsʌbtaɪtlz/
incredible   /ɪnˈkredəbl/
incredibly   /ɪnˈkredəbli/
dress (well)   /ˈdres/
a strong accent   /ə strɒŋ ˈæksent/
first impressions   /fɜːst ɪmˈpreʃnz/
get dark   /get ˈdɑːk/
in general   /ɪn ˈdʒenrəl/
lock (your) doors   /lɒk ˈdɔːz/

> I'd love to live like a poor man, but with lots of money.
>
> Pablo Picasso, Spanish painter

11B What do you want to do?

1 GRAMMAR verbs + to + infinitive

a Complete the sentences with *to* and a verb in the box.

| become cook download go ride spend |
| stop visit |

1. I'd like _to go_ on a safari.
2. My brother's learning _____ a motorbike.
3. Do you need _____ less time on your computer?
4. She wants _____ biting her nails.
5. Would you like _____ New York?
6. We know all their songs, so we don't need _____ the lyrics.
7. I'm leaving home next month so I need to learn _____ a meal.
8. Do you want _____ a singer?

b Write sentences or questions with *would like*. Use contractions.

1. he / have very long hair [−]
   He wouldn't like to have very long hair.
2. you / climb a mountain [?]
   _____?
3. we / get up earlier [+]
   _____.
4. I / learn to fly a plane [+]
   _____.
5. she / make a short film [−]
   _____.
6. they / get married [?]
   _____?

2 VOCABULARY verbs that take the infinitive

Match the sentences 1–8 with the sentences a–h.

1. I'm having some lessons. [f]
2. Our washing machine is broken. ☐
3. I have a lot of dresses. ☐
4. I'm playing tennis tomorrow. ☐
5. That girl is Brazilian so I can't speak to her. ☐
6. We are looking at hotels in the South of France. ☐
7. I don't have time to do my homework now. ☐
8. I'm in love with my boyfriend. ☐

a I'd like to learn Portuguese.
b I promise to do it later.
c I hope to win the match.
d We want to get married.
e We're planning to go there on holiday.
f ~~I'm learning to drive.~~
g We need to buy a new one.
h I decided to wear the red one.

3 PRONUNCIATION sentence stress

a Underline the stressed words.

1. **A** Would you like to drive a sports car?
   B Yes, I'd love to.
   A Why?
   B Because I love cars and I love driving.
2. **A** Would you like to ride a horse?
   B No, I wouldn't.
   A Why not?
   B Because I don't like horses.
3. **A** Do you want to learn to cook?
   B Yes, I need to.
   A Why?
   B Because I want to live on my own.

b iChecker Listen and check. Then listen and repeat the dialogues.

71

4 LISTENING

a **iChecker** Listen to a TV presenter interviewing three people about things they want to do with their lives. What are their ambitions?

1 Dave

2 Sandy

3 Eddie

b **iChecker** Listen again and write T (true) or F (false).
1 Dave had a Triumph motorbike when he was younger. __
2 Dave has a girlfriend. __
3 Sandy is planning to visit Canada with her boyfriend. __
4 Sandy enjoys flying. __
5 Eddie has tickets to see his favourite band in concert. __
6 Kings of Leon aren't touring this year. __

USEFUL WORDS AND PHRASES

Learn these words and phrases.

ambitions /æmˈbɪʃnz/
recipes /ˈresəpiz/
preferably /ˈprefrəbli/
serious /ˈsɪəriəs/
translate /trænzˈleɪt/
be yourself /bi jɔːˈself/
bite your nails /baɪt jɔː ˈneɪlz/
(see a band) live /laɪv/
stay awake /steɪ əˈweɪk/

5 READING

a Read the text. Answer the questions with **J** (Jacques), **K** (Kimberley), **Y** (Yusuke), or **G** (Giulio).

Things I want to do

Jacques, 25, France
I'd love to be in Times Square in New York at midnight on New Year's Eve! And I'd like it to be snowing too – that's more romantic. People say that the atmosphere there is amazing. I think it would be a great experience.

Kimberley, 31, Canada
I want to visit the Amazon rainforest. It's such a unique and fascinating place and I'm really interested in the wildlife that lives there. I'd like to do a trek and go camping there for three weeks or so. I've seen a lot of films about explorers and now I'd like to do something really exciting myself.

Yusuke, 26, Japan
What I want to do is go on a road trip across Europe with my two best friends. I've been to the US and Canada, but I've never been to Europe. I want to see all the famous tourist sites like the Eiffel Tower, Big Ben, and the Leaning Tower of Pisa. I read about them in books when I was a child – it would be a dream come true for me to see them in real life.

Giulio, 34, Italy
It's not very original, but I'd like to drive a really expensive, classic sports car through the Alps with my girlfriend next to me in the passenger seat. However, at the moment I own a Fiat Punto, so I may have to wait a few years before I can achieve my dream!

1 Which person became interested in their dream when they were very young? ☐
2 Who wants to be part of a traditional celebration? ☐
3 Who needs to buy something before they can achieve their dream? ☐
4 Which person would like a bit of adventure? ☐

b Guess the meaning of the highlighted words. Check the meaning and pronunciation in your dictionary.

72

11C Men, women, and the internet

> I had a life once...now I have a computer.
> *Anonymous*

1 GRAMMAR articles

a Correct the mistake in each answer (**B**).

1. A Where are the children? B They're at ~~the~~ school.
2. A What do you do? B I'm engineer.
3. A Where's the juice? B In a fridge.
4. A What's that? B A identity card.
5. A How often do you go? B Twice the week.
6. A What animals do you like? B I like the dogs.
7. A How did you travel? B By a train.
8. A Where did you book? B On internet.

b Complete the text with *the*, *a / an*, or –.

Most people think that [1] *the* internet is a good thing. At [2] _____ work, employees can use it to search for [3] _____ information and to send and receive [4] _____ emails. At [5] _____ home, [6] _____ people can use it for entertainment. You can watch [7] _____ music videos, listen to [8] _____ music or, play [9] _____ latest computer games online. It is also useful for [10] _____ shopping, and you don't have to go to [11] _____ bank if you have [12] _____ online banking service. However, there are some dangers because there is [13] _____ problem with security. [14] _____ computer virus can break your computer and [15] _____ computer hackers can steal your identity.

2 VOCABULARY The internet

Unscramble the words to complete the sentences.

1. All our hotel rooms have __Wi-fi__ (IW-IF) access.
2. It's cheaper to _____ (PKSEY) than to make a phone call.
3. Do you ever shop _____ (NONELI)?
4. You only need your username and your password to _____ (GOL NI).
5. Do you want to _____ (DLWODNAO) this file?
6. I sometimes forget to include the _____ (TATHCANEMT) in my emails.
7. I need to _____ (RASHEC ROF) some information before I write my report.
8. You can _____ (OGLEGO) the name of the restaurant to find out the address.
9. They're going to _____ (POLUDA) their holiday photos tonight.

3 PRONUNCIATION word stress

a Under<u>line</u> the stressed syllable in these words.

1	email	network	website
2	address	online	results
3	document	internet	username
4	attachment	computer	directions

b **iChecker** Listen and check. Then listen and repeat the words.

73

4 READING

a Read the article. When did the World Wide Web begin? _____

b Read the article again and number the events in the order they happened.

- [ ] Tim Berners-Lee developed a new computer language.
- [ ] The Americans opened an agency to develop new technology.
- [ ] They put the new language on the internet.
- [1] The Russians sent a satellite into space.
- [ ] The World Wide Web made the internet available to all computer users.
- [ ] The network changed its name to the internet.
- [ ] The agency developed a network to connect computers.
- [ ] Berners-Lee and a colleague used the new language to write a new program.

5 LISTENING

a iChecker Listen to four speakers talking about how they use the internet. Match speakers 1–4 to the thing they do most often.

Speaker [ ] uses a social network.
Speaker [ ] plays games.
Speaker [ ] does a job.
Speaker [ ] talks to family and friends.

b iChecker Listen again and match the speakers to the sentences A–D.

Speaker 1 [ ]   Speaker 3 [ ]
Speaker 2 [ ]   Speaker 4 [ ]

A This person often puts photos on the internet.
B This person likes his / her job.
C This person uses the internet to relax.
D This person saves money because of the internet.

USEFUL WORDS AND PHRASES

Learn these words and phrases.

advice /ədˈvaɪs/
both /bəʊθ/
password /ˈpɑːswɜːd/
username /ˈjuːzəneɪm/
book (tickets / hotels) /bʊk/
lose weight /luːz ˈweɪt/
make transfers /meɪk ˈtrænsfɜːz/
online shopping /ɒnlaɪn ˈʃɒpɪŋ/
pay bills /peɪ ˈbɪlz/

The story behind the World Wide Web

To find out when the World Wide Web began, we first need to look at the internet. The origins of the internet go back to the Space Race of the 1950s. After the Russians sent the satellite Sputnik into space, the Americans wanted to develop their own technology further, so they set up ARPA – the Advanced Research Projects Agency. This agency found a way of connecting computers, which they called ARPANET. In 1974, they changed its name to 'the internetwork' or 'internet' for short.

In 1980, a scientist at CERN, the European Organization for Nuclear Research, wrote a computer program so that he and his colleagues could share their research. The scientist's name was Tim Berners-Lee, and his software was called ENQUIRE. At first, only scientists at CERN could use the program, which contained a new computer language called hypertext. Then, in 1991, he and a colleague wrote a more advanced version of the program which made hypertext available over the internet. This was the beginning of the World Wide Web, as we know it. The first website and web server was info.cern.ch. Today, there are more than 227 million websites containing over 65 billion web pages.

Over two billion people now use the internet, which is nearly a third of the world's population.

 FILE 11

Practical English Going home

1 VOCABULARY Public transport

Complete the paragraphs.

1 You can get a taxi or a ¹ _cab_ at a taxi ² r_____. People usually give the driver a ³ t_____.

2 Before you get a plane, you have to ⁴ ch_____ in online or at the airport. Then you go through security to the ⁵ d_____ lounge. Finally you go to your ⁶ g_____.

3 You get a train at a railway ⁷ st_____. First you get a ⁸ t_____ and then you find the right ⁹ pl_____.

4 You get a bus or a ¹⁰ c_____ at a bus station. You can also get a bus at a bus ¹¹ st_____. You can buy a ticket in advance or sometimes you can pay the ¹² dr_____.

2 GETTING TO THE AIRPORT

Complete the conversations with a sentence in the box.

Can I pay by credit card?
~~Could you call me a taxi, please?~~
Could I have a ticket to Luton Airport, please?
How much is it?   And could I have a receipt?
Now, please.   Single, please.
Standard, please.   To St Pancras station.

1 A ¹ _Could you call me a taxi, please?_
   B Yes, of course. Where to?
   A ² _____
   B And when would you like it for?
   A ³ _____

2 A ⁴ _____
   C That's £18.50, please.
   A Make it £20. ⁵ _____
   C Thank you very much, sir.

3 A ⁶ _____
   D Single or return?
   A ⁷ _____
   D Standard or first class?
   A ⁸ _____
   D That's £18.50.
   A ⁹ _____
   D Yes, of course.

3 SOCIAL ENGLISH

Match the words to make phrases.

1 I can't   [e]   a to accept.
2 Thank you   [ ]   b good journey.
3 I'd love   [ ]   c in London.
4 I'm so   [ ]   d so much.
5 Have a   [ ]   e ~~believe it!~~
6 See you   [ ]   f happy.

4 READING

a Read the text about Gatwick Airport.

Gatwick Airport

Gatwick Airport is London's second-largest international airport and 31.3 million passengers pass through it every year. Below you can find different ways of getting to the airport.

BY CAR
If you're planning to drive to Gatwick Airport, you need to take the M23 motorway and turn off at Junction 9. The airport is 45 km from London and five minutes from the nearest town, Crawley.

BY BIKE
The National Cycle Network Route will take you to the airport, where you can leave your bike in a special cycle parking area. Take National Route 21 to the South Terminal, and then take the lift into the terminal building.

BY TRAIN
The Gatwick Express runs every fifteen minutes and takes only half an hour from Victoria Station in Central London. A single ticket bought on the day costs £17.95, but tickets are cheaper if you buy them online.

BY BUS OR COACH
EasyBus operates a service to the airport from Earl's Court in the centre of London which runs all day and all night. The buses run every 15 minutes, and drop you off in front of the terminal buildings. The price for a single ticket can be as low as £2, but you need to book early.

BY TAXI
Phone Airport Cars 24 hours a day for a taxi to take you to Gatwick Airport. The cost of a taxi from Central London to the airport is £95, and the journey takes about an hour.

b How did the following people get to Gatwick Airport?

1 Chris made a phone call.   By _taxi_____.
2 Emma paid £2.   By _____.
3 Debbie went from Victoria Station. By _____.
4 Pete went on the motorway.   By _____.
5 Harry did some exercise.   By _____.

c Underline five words or phrases you don't know. Use your dictionary to look up their meaning and pronunciation.

12A Books and films

Films should have a beginning, a middle, and an end – but not necessarily in that order.
Jean-Luc Godard, French film director

1 GRAMMAR present perfect

a Write the sentences with contractions.

1 I have not read *The Pillars of the Earth*.
   I haven't read The Pillars of the Earth.
2 James has not seen this film before.
   _____
3 They have gone to the cinema tonight.
   _____
4 She has cried in a lot of films.
   _____
5 I have bought all the Harry Potter films.
   _____
6 They have not taken any photos.
   _____
7 He has interviewed a famous actor.
   _____
8 We have not appeared in a film.
   _____

b Write sentences with the present perfect.

1 she / read / *Jane Eyre*
   She's read Jane Eyre .
2 we / not see / this programme
   We haven't seen this programme .
3 my parents / fall asleep
   _____ .
4 Adam / appear / in a film
   _____ .
5 I / not speak to an actor
   _____ .
6 you / break / the camera
   _____ .
7 Dawn / not cry / in a film
   _____ .
8 we / not forget / the tickets
   _____ .

c Complete the dialogue.

A ¹ *Have you heard* (you / hear) of John le Carré?
B Yes, I ² _____ (read) some of his books.
A Really? Which books ³ _____ (you / read)
B I ⁴ _____ (read) *The Constant Gardener* recently. It was great!
A ⁵ _____ (you / see) the film?
B No, but my boyfriend ⁶ _____ (see) it. He loves John le Carré.
A ⁷ _____ (he / read) *Tinker, Tailor, Soldier, Spy*?
B Yes, and we ⁸ _____ (see) the film.

2 VOCABULARY irregular past participles

a Write the past simple forms and past participles of these irregular verbs in the chart.

Infinitive	Past simple	Past participle
1 be	was / were	been
2 break		
3 do		
4 eat		
5 fall		
6 forget		
7 go		
8 leave		
9 speak		
10 sing		
11 take		
12 wear		

b Use past participles from the chart in a to complete the sentences.

1 Have you ever *sung* karaoke?
2 We've never _____ the cinema before the end of a film.
3 My girlfriend has never _____ octopus before.
4 Has your boyfriend ever _____ your birthday?
5 Have you ever _____ glasses?
6 I've never _____ my leg.
7 My friend hasn't _____ the homework.

76

3 PRONUNCIATION sentence stress

a **iChecker** Listen and underline the stressed words.

A Have you read *The Millennium Trilogy*?
B No, I haven't.
A Have you seen the films?
B Yes, I have. I've seen all of them.

b **iChecker** Listen again and repeat the sentences. Copy the rhythm.

4 READING

a Read the article about a film adaptation of a book. Did fans prefer the ending in the book or the film?

Fans of American author Jodi Picoult who have read her novel *My Sister's Keeper* get a big surprise when they see the film. This is because the film has a completely different ending from the book.

The novel tells the story of 13-year-old Anna Fitzgerald who was born to save the life of her older sister, Kate, who is very ill. Kate has cancer and Anna goes to hospital many times to give her sister blood and other things to keep Kate alive. However, when Anna is 13, she finds out that Kate needs one of her kidneys and she decides that she doesn't want to give it to her. Anna goes to find a lawyer to help her fight her case in court.

At the end of the book, Anna wins her case so that in the future she can make her own decisions about her body. Unfortunately, the same day as she wins the case, she is in her lawyer's car when they have a serious accident. Anna is brain-dead after the crash, and the lawyer gives the doctors permission to use Anna's kidney. So in the end, Anna dies and Kate lives.

At the end of the film, before they know the result of the court case, Kate and Anna's brother, Jesse, tells the family that Kate doesn't want to have any more operations. Kate dies and then Anna's lawyer visits the house to tell Anna she has won the case. So, in the film Kate dies and Anna lives.

A website asked the people who have read the book and seen the film to vote on the two different endings. 77% said that they hated the new ending while 13% said they preferred it to the ending in the book. Ten percent said that they enjoyed both the book and the film and that the ending made no difference to them.

b Read the article again and choose a, b, or c.

1 Jodi Picoult is…
   a a lawyer.
   b a writer.
   c a doctor.
2 Anna's parents had Anna because…
   a they wanted another child.
   b they wanted to save their daughter.
   c they wanted another girl.
3 …dies at the end of the book.
   a The healthy sister
   b The sister who was ill
   c The brother
4 … dies at the end of the film.
   a The healthy sister
   b The sister who was ill
   c The brother
5 … of the people who voted didn't think the ending was important.
   a 77%
   b 13%
   c 10%

5 LISTENING

a **iChecker** Listen to a radio programme. Who wrote the two books? _____

b **iChecker** Listen again. Write T (true) or F (false).
1 *Great Expectations* was made in 1956.   F
2 The film critic is going to talk about two films.   __
3 *Great Expectations* is a black and white film.   __
4 The main character in *Great Expectations* is a girl.   __
5 The film is more frightening than the book.   __
6 The presenter has read the book *The English Patient*.   __
7 The author of *The English Patient* isn't British.   __
8 The main character in *The English Patient* had a car crash.   __
9 The critic says that the best thing about the film is the love story.   __
10 Both the book and the film have won important prizes.   __

USEFUL WORDS AND PHRASES

Learn these words and phrases.

blood /blʌd/
appear /əˈpɪə/
a bit (tired) /ə bɪt/
at least /ət ˈliːst/
fall asleep /fɔːl əˈsliːp/
How about…? /ˈhaʊ əbaʊt/
order pizza /ˈɔːdə ˈpiːtsə/

12B I've never been there!

> I want to go somewhere I have never been, and I'd like to go there with you.
> From *The Hitchhiker's Guide to the Galaxy* by Douglas Adams, British writer

1 GRAMMAR present perfect or past simple?

a Complete the dialogues with the correct form of the verbs in brackets.

1. **A** _Have you been_ (you / be) on holiday recently?
   B Yes, we have. We _____ (go) to the beach in July.
2. **A** When _____ (your brother / buy) his motorbike?
   B Last week. My parents _____ (pay) for it.
3. **A** _____ (you / meet) your sister's new boyfriend?
   B Yes, I _____ (meet) him at a party last month.
4. **A** _____ (you / be) to New York?
   B Yes, I _____ (go) there last year.
5. **A** _____ (your parents / ever / give) you an expensive present?
   B Yes, I _____ (have) a car for my last birthday.
6. **A** Why _____ (he / send) his wife some flowers yesterday?
   B Because he _____ (forget) their anniversary.

b Complete the sentences with *gone* or *been*.

1. Has Clare _gone_ home? She isn't at her desk.
2. Have you ever _____ to Disneyland?
3. My sister isn't here because she's _____ for a walk.
4. My neighbours are away because they've _____ on holiday.
5. You look brown. Have you _____ to the beach?
6. It's late so the children have _____ to bed.
7. The cupboards are full because we've _____ shopping.
8. Have you ever _____ to an Indian restaurant?
9. My girlfriend has never _____ abroad.
10. Jane's parents are out. They've _____ to the supermarket.

2 PRONUNCIATION irregular past participles

a Circle the word with a different vowel sound.

1 fish	2 horse	3 egg	4 up	5 train	6 phone
given	found	left	come	taken	broken
written	thought	heard	done	made	known
seen	caught	said	drunk	read	lost
driven	worn	sent	got	paid	spoken

b iChecker Listen and check. Then listen and repeat the words.

3 VOCABULARY more irregular past participles

a Write the past simple forms and past participles of these irregular verbs in the chart.

Infinitive	Past simple	Past participle
1 buy	*bought*	*bought*
2 drink		
3 find		
4 give		
5 have		
6 hear		
7 know		
8 lose		
9 make		
10 meet		
11 pay		
12 send		
13 spend		
14 think		
15 win		

b Complete the sentences with past participles from the chart in **a**.

1. I'm going to be late. I've _lost_ the car keys.
2. Have you ever _____ long hair?
3. Debbie and Fernando have _____ a new house.
4. Jamie can't go out because he's _____ all his money.
5. My parents have never _____ of U2.
6. You've _____ a lot of mistakes.
7. She's _____ some money in the street.
8. He's _____ a lot of water today because it's so hot.

78

4 READING

a Read the email. What is the relationship between Becky and Joanne? _____

Schönbrunn Palace, Vienna

From: Joanne
To: Becky
Subject: Hi from Europe!

Dear Becky,

Thanks for your email telling me all the news from home. I'm glad everyone is well and that you're not missing me too much!

We're about half way through our trip around Europe and we're having a great time. We've stayed in four countries so far and now we're in Croatia. We've been to Germany, the Czech Republic, Austria, and Hungary. We spent three days in Berlin where we went on the free New Berlin walking tour which took us to the Brandenburg Gate. From Berlin we went to Prague where we spent another three days seeing the sights. We even watched a ballet one evening in one of Prague's many theatres. Our next stop was Vienna which we found quite expensive. The best part of our visit was the Schönbrunn Palace. From Vienna we went to Budapest, where we decided to relax and enjoy a spa. The weather was beautiful in Budapest, and there is a lot to see. We wanted to stay longer, but it was time for us to go to Croatia. And here we are now in Split. Split is a lovely place with lots of historic buildings. We've been to the beach today, but unfortunately it rained – just our luck!

We have one more day in Croatia and then we're going to get the train to Venice. We haven't been to Italy or Greece yet, so we're looking forward to the last part of our trip.

I'll write again when we get to Athens. Until then, take care and give my love to Mum and Dad.

Lots of love

Joanne

b Read the email again and complete the sentences with the words from the box.

a ballet   the beach   ~~the Brandenburg Gate~~
Italy or Greece   the Schönbrunn Palace   a spa

1 Joanne has seen _the Brandenburg Gate_ in Berlin.
2 She's watched _____ in Prague.
3 She's visited _____ in Vienna.
4 She's been to _____ in Budapest.
5 She's been to _____ in Split.
6 She hasn't been to _____.

5 LISTENING

a **iChecker** Listen to four speakers talking about different places they have been to. Where did they go? When?

	Where?	When?
Speaker 1	_____	_____
Speaker 2	_____	_____
Speaker 3	_____	_____
Speaker 4	_____	_____

b **iChecker** Listen again. Who…?

1 did an extreme sport   Speaker ☐
2 was in a dangerous situation Speaker ☐
3 took part in a local celebration Speaker ☐
4 wasn't on holiday   Speaker ☐

USEFUL WORDS AND PHRASES

Learn these words and phrases.

recently /ˈriːsntli/
romantic /rəʊˈmæntɪk/
Let's forget it. /lets fəˈɡet ɪt/
TV series /tiː ˈviː sɪəriːz/
win (a cup or medal) /wɪn/

> One Ring to rule them all, One Ring to find them,
> One Ring to bring them all and in the darkness bind them.
> From The Fellowship of the Ring by J R R Tolkien, British author

12C The *English File* questionnaire

1 GRAMMAR revision

a Correct the mistakes in the second sentence.

1 Those are her children. They is very young.
   They are very young.
2 Jim lives in the city centre. Your flat is very big.
   _____
3 I went shopping yesterday. I bought a shirt new.
   _____
4 That's Sophie. She's the girlfriend of Ryan.
   _____
5 We love the summer. We go on holiday on August.
   _____
6 Tanya is going to lose her job. She always is late.
   _____
7 I don't like karaoke. I can't to sing.
   _____
8 My boyfriend is late. I'm waiting for he.
   _____
9 We're doing the housework. We don't mind clean.
   _____
10 Our garden is small. There aren't some plants.
   _____
11 The hotel was full. There was a lot of guests.
   _____
12 They're quite healthy. They don't eat many sugar.
   _____
13 I'm 21. I'm more older than you.
   _____
14 I don't like crocodiles. They're the more dangerous animals.
   _____
15 Hannah likes languages. She speaks German good.
   _____
16 My sister has a good job. She's engineer.
   _____

b Look at the **time expressions** and complete the sentences with the correct form of the verbs. Use the present simple, present continuous, past simple, present perfect, or *be going to*.

1 We **never** _have_ pizza for dinner. (have)
2 Caitlin _____ the dog for a walk **twice a day**. (take)
3 _____ you _____ your friends **last weekend**? (see)
4 They _____ **tomorrow** because Jack is ill. (not come)
5 _____ you **ever** _____ to South America? (be)
6 _____ your son _____ drive **next year**? (learn)
7 We _____ meat **every day**. (not eat)
8 We _____ a film **next Saturday**. (see)
9 _____ you **ever** _____ a famous person? (meet)
10 **Last night** my husband _____ dinner. (cook)
11 I think it _____ **tonight**. (rain)
12 What time _____ you **usually** _____ to bed at the weekend? (go)
13 My boyfriend _____ football **at the moment**. (play)
14 We _____ to work **yesterday**. (not walk)
15 What _____ your daughter _____ **today**? (do)
16 I _____ **never** _____ that book, but I'd like to. (read)

2 VOCABULARY revision: word groups

a (Circle) the word that is different.

1 Hungary	(Japanese)	Turkey	China
2 Egypt	Switzerland	Asia	Mexico
3 tall	expensive	dark	slim
4 builder	hairdresser	cooker	waiter
5 aunt	daughter	niece	brother
6 spring	cloudy	snowy	windy
7 fireplace	cupboard	sofa	kitchen
8 mushroom	strawberries	onion	peas
9 chemist's	department store	bridge	shopping mall

b Continue the series.

1 one, two, three, _four_
2 ten, twenty, _____
3 Monday, Tuesday, _____
4 first, second, _____
5 morning, afternoon, _____
6 once, twice, _____
7 summer, autumn, _____
8 June, July, _____
9 second, minute, _____
10 day, week, _____

c Complete the phrases with verbs.

1 _listen_ to music
2 d_____ exercise
3 s_____ hello
4 h_____ a shower
5 g_____ shopping
6 t_____ photos
7 h_____ a noise
8 g_____ dressed
9 h_____ two children
10 u_____ a computer

80

3 PRONUNCIATION revision: sounds

a Circle the word with a different sound.

fish /ɪ/	1	rich dirty big
tree /iː/	2	bread peas meat
cat /æ/	3	safe black fat
car /ɑː/	4	dark day far
clock /ɒ/	5	money model doctor
horse /ɔː/	6	found short bought
bull /ʊ/	7	cook food good
boot /uː/	8	who do go
bird /ɜː/	9	tired thirsty nurse
egg /e/	10	eat healthy breakfast
train /eɪ/	11	paid steak said
bike /aɪ/	12	buy nice ring

b iChecker Listen and check.

c Underline the stressed syllable.

1 hos|pi|tal
2 ex|pen|sive
3 ma|ga|zine
4 head|phones
5 ad|min|is|tra|tor
6 en|gi|neer
7 I|tal|ian
8 Au|gust
9 di|ffi|cult
10 mu|si|cian
11 ga|rage
12 ba|na|nas

d iChecker Listen and check.

4 READING

Read the article and answer the questions.

THE FILMS in *The Lord of the Rings* trilogy have had a big impact on New Zealand. The country has become 'Middle Earth' to many of the people who have seen the films. This comes as no surprise to the film director Peter Jackson, who is in fact a New Zealander. He chose his home country because he knew that the variety of different landscapes made New Zealand the best place to shoot the films.

Jackson and his team looked over the whole country for the most beautiful and most appropriate areas. The rolling hills of Matamata became Hobbiton, the village where Bilbo Baggins lives, and the volcanic region of Mount Ruapehu transformed into the fiery Mount Doom, where Sauron first made the Ring. In total, the team used 150 different locations all over New Zealand and they spent 274 days filming.

Thirty of the locations Jackson used are National Parks or conservation sites so he needed to get special permission to film here. In some cases, a special team dug up the protected plants, and took them to special nurseries, where they lived until filming finished. Then the team took them back to the park and replanted them again. In Queenstown, Jackson used enormous red carpets to protect the plants in the battle scenes because there were up to 1,100 people on set every day.

The *Lord of the Rings* films have been so popular that the tourist industry in New Zealand has grown dramatically. Today, tour companies offer a wide range of tours to different locations of the film, including Hobbiton, Mount Doom, and Edoras.

1 Who directed *The Lord of the Rings* films?
2 Where is the director from?
3 Why did he choose New Zealand?
4 Which area did they use to create Mount Doom?
5 How many different locations did they use in total?
6 What was the problem with some of the locations?
7 How did they solve the problem?
8 Which locations from the films can tourists visit today?

5 LISTENING

iChecker Listen to an advert for a day trip and complete the notes.

Lord of the Rings Edoras Tour

Departure time:	Christchurch ¹ _9 a.m._	Lunch:	luxury ⁵_____
Return time:	Christchurch ²_____	Price:	
Transport:	by ³_____	Adults:	⁶ $_____
Destination:	Mount ⁴_____ (Edoras)	Children:	⁷ $_____

iChecker TESTS **FILE 12**

81

Listening

1 A

1
Nick Hello.
Sophie Hi Nick.
Nick Hi Sophie.
Sophie Nick, what's Sarah's phone number?
Nick Erm…It's 161 496 542.
Sophie Thank you!

2
Receptionist OK…your class on Tuesday is with Paul, and it's in room two. Your class on Thursday is with Kate, and it's in room five.
Student OK, so Thursday is in room three, and Tuesday in room five?
Receptionist No – it's Tuesday in room two, and Thursday in room five.

3
Liz A ham sandwich and a coffee, please.
Barista That's five dollars twenty, please. Thank you.
Liz Thank you.
Barista Have a nice day!

1 B

1 A Are you Russian?
   B No, I'm Polish. I'm from Kraków.
2 A Where are you from?
   B We're American. We're from California. We're on holiday in Europe.
3 A Where's he from? Is he Spanish?
   B No, he isn't. He's from Mexico. He's from Cancún.
4 A Mmmm, delicious. Is it French?
   B No, it isn't. It's Italian.

1 C

R = Receptionist, E = Erik
R Good morning. Can I help you?
E Oh, yes. Hello. I have a reservation.
R OK. What's your name?
E Erik.
R Is that Eric with a C?
E No, it's with a K. E-R-I-K.
R Right. And how do you spell your surname?
E T-A-Y-L-O-R
R Can you repeat that please?
E Yes, of course. Sorry. T-A-Y-L-O-R.
R Thanks. Now just a few questions, Mr Taylor. Where are you from?
E I'm from Australia.
R Where in Australia?
E Perth.
R Perth. OK. And what's your address?
E It's 15 Atkinson Road.
R What's your postcode?
E Sorry?
R The postcode. You know, a number?
E Ah yes. It's WA 6008.
R 6008. Great. What's your email address?
E It's eriktaylor@mail.com.
R And what's your phone number?
E My phone number in Perth is 61 – that's the code for Australia – 08 7010 5692.
R 61 08 7010 5692.
E Yes, that's right. And my mobile number is 61 491 570 156.
R 61 491 570 156. Right, thanks. Mr Taylor. Here's your keycard. You're in room 305 on the third floor. Enjoy your stay.
E Thank you very much.

2 A

Speaker 1 My bag is very important to me because I have my laptop in it! I also have some files and a pen. Um, I have my mobile, my wallet, and my keys in my pocket, but I sometimes have a newspaper in my bag.
Speaker 2 Well, in my bag I have, er, my books for the day, um, some pens and pencils to write with, and a file with lots of paper. Oh, and I have my iPod and my headphones too, so I can listen to music.
Speaker 3 What's in my bag? Well, yeah, I have my sunglasses and my camera. And I have a guidebook with a map. Oh, and I have a Spanish-English dictionary, too, to help me understand the people.
Speaker 4 I have a different bag every day, sometimes it's red, sometimes it's white, it depends. But I always have the same things: some tissues, um, the keys to my desk, er, my purse of course, and, er, sometimes a magazine to read.

2 B

1 He's a Hollywood star but he isn't American. He's very tall and slim. He's about 54 or 55 I think, but he's still very attractive. He has short brown hair and brown eyes. He's an actor.
2 She's quite young and she isn't very tall. She's usually quite slim but it depends. Her hair is really brown, but it's blonde in her music videos. She's American and she's a singer.
3 This actor isn't very tall, but he's very strong. He has short dark hair and dark eyes. He's American and I think he's nearly 70 years old.
4 She's about 54 or 55 now and she's quite tall and slim. She has blonde hair, sometimes long and sometimes short, and green eyes. She's a British actress and she's in some of the Harry Potter films.
5 He's a British singer and musician. He's about 62 or 63 now, I think. He's quite slim. He has short blonde hair, and blue eyes. He is also an actor.

2 C

1 A I'm bored.
  B Me, too.
  A I know! Let's watch a DVD.
  B Good idea.
  A We can watch the new Batman film.
  B OK.
  A Turn on the TV, then. Now…where's the film?
2 A I'm hungry.
  B Are you?
  A Yes, I am. Is the restaurant open?
  B No, it isn't. It's only five o'clock.
  A Oh.
  B Let's call reception. We can ask for some sandwiches.
  A Great idea! Give me the phone.
3 A I'm hot.
  B Turn on the air conditioning, then.
  A It's already on.
  B Is it? OK, then let's open the windows.
  A Are we nearly there?
  B Yes, we are. Don't worry. It's only another 20 kilometres.
4 B I'm not hungry.
  A Why not?
  B I'm stressed. I have a lot of problems at work.
  A Relax! It's the weekend. Let's go for a long walk and you can tell me all about it.
  B Right.
  A Finish your salad and we can go.
  B OK. Let's pay the bill.
5 A I'm tired.
  B I know. It's quite late.
  A What time is our plane?
  B At 23.15. That's another hour to wait.
  A An hour!
  B Yes. Come on. Let's have a coffee. It might wake us up.

3 A

Hannah I like the parks in Britain, especially Hyde Park in London. The parks are clean and some are really big, and it's great to go for a walk and see so many trees and plants in the middle of a city. There is always something interesting to see or do, too. Sometimes there are festivals where you can hear music or watch a film. But I can also relax, and read a newspaper on a Sunday morning.
 But, I don't like the food here – it's very expensive, and I can't find good Korean food!
Anna In Britain, I think that people are very friendly and polite, more than in Poland where I am from. At work, it's quite relaxed, and my colleagues always help me when I have a question or a problem. I also really like the buildings in Britain; the old buildings are very beautiful.
 What don't I like about Britain? There are a lot of people and a lot of traffic, especially in London. It's difficult to relax.
Roberta What I really like about Britain is that it's really easy to meet people from all over the world. It's very international, and I think that most people are friendly to people from other countries. I also really like eating food from different parts of the world – in Britain you can try food from every country!
 I think it's difficult to make friends in Britain. People like to help and are very polite, but it can take a long time to become friends with British people.

3 B

P = Presenter, J = James, H = Helen, F = Frank
P Good evening and welcome to What's your job? And our team tonight are Helen, who's a lawyer…
H Good evening.
P …and Frank, who's an actor.
F Good evening.
P And our first guest tonight is…
J James.

P Hello James. OK team, you have one minute to ask James questions about his job, starting now. Let's have your first question.
H James, do you make things?
J No. No, I don't.
F James, do you have special qualifications?
J Yes, I do. Qualifications from university.
H Do you speak any foreign languages?
J No, I don't need any foreign languages.
F Do you wear a uniform?
J Well, it's not really a uniform, but I wear a white coat, yes.
H Do you travel?
J Er, I don't go to different countries, but I drive to people's houses sometimes.
F Do you earn a lot of money?
J Do I earn a lot of money? Well, I think the money is quite good, yes.
P You only have time for one more question, team.
H Do you work with other people?
J Well, I work with one other person, but my job isn't really about people…
P That's time. OK, team. So, what's James's job?

3 C

J = Jessica, M = Max
J Hi. Are you Max?
M Yes. Are you Jessica?
J Yes, I am.
M Nice to meet you. Well, let's go in and sit down. Do you like sushi?
J Yes. I love Japanese food. It's my favourite.
M Good. So, Jessica, what do you do?
J I'm a flight attendant.
M Really? That's incredible?
J Why?
M Because I'm a pilot!
J Oh! You're right. That is incredible! Which airline do you work for?
M KLM. And you?
J British Airways. I love my job.
M Me too. What do you do at the weekend, Jessica?
J I meet my friends. We go to the cinema or to a restaurant. How about you?
M I like the cinema, too. What kind of films do you like?
J I like comedies more than anything.
M Me too. Who's your favourite actor?
J Johnny Depp. I love him!
M Yes, he's good, isn't he? Do you live near the cinema?
J Yes, there's a cinema near my house.
M When do you go there?
J I go on Saturday evenings.
M Let's go together next Saturday.
J OK. What do you want to see?

4 A

A = Angie, J = Jessie
A Who's that?
J That's my nephew.
A Is that your sister's son or your brother's son?
J My brother's.
A How old is your nephew? He looks quite young.
J He's 13. The photo is from his birthday last week.
A Let's see the next one. Is that your family, too?
J Yes, it is. That's my sister.
A Wow! She's really tall.
J Yes, she plays basketball. She's quite good.
A That's a beautiful beach. Where is it?
J It's a beach in Menorca – I can't remember the name. I love it there!
A Is this Menorca, too?
J No, it isn't. It's a music festival in Germany.

A Are those girls in your family?
J No, they aren't. They're friends from university.
A Who's the blonde one?
J That's Rosie. We live in the same flat.
A Who's the boy?
J He's Rosie's boyfriend. I don't like him very much, but she doesn't often see him.
A Are there any more?
J Yes. Have a look at this one.
A You look great! And who's that sitting next to you?
J He's my boyfriend, Pete. It's the office party from last year.
A He's attractive. Does he work with you?
J Well, sort of…He's the manager!

4 B

I = Interviewer, M = Mark
I What do you do, Mark?
M I'm a taxi driver.
I Do you work at night or during the day?
M I work at night.
I What time do you start work?
M At about seven o'clock in the evening. I stop for a break at about two o'clock and I have something to eat.
I What do you have?
M A hamburger or a pizza and a coke. I'm very hungry at that time.
I What time do you finish work, Mark?
M I go home at about six o'clock in the morning and I go to bed immediately. I sleep for about eight hours and then I get up and have breakfast.
I What do you do in the afternoon?
M I go to the gym for an hour or so, and then I have a shower. After that, I watch TV or check my emails until I have dinner.
I What time is that?
M At six o'clock. Then I get into my car and start work again.
I Do you like your job?
M Yes, I love it.
I Thank you for your time, Mark.
M You're welcome.

4 C

P = Presenter, M = Marge,
R = Robbie, D = Dr Atkins
P Hello and welcome to Who's healthy? Today we have Marge Wilson and her son, Robbie, with us. Marge, do you think you're healthy?
M Um, yes. I think so.
P And what about you, Robbie? Are you healthy?
R Of course!
P Well, I'm going to ask you some questions and we're going to find out who's healthy. First of all, Marge. How old are you, Marge?
M I'm 48.
P Right. So, how often do you eat fast food, Marge?
M Never. I don't like it.
P Right. And how often do you have breakfast?
M I always have breakfast. I have a cup of tea and some cereal.
P Good. And how often do you do exercise?
M I go to the gym three times a week.
P OK, and how many hours do you usually sleep?
M Well, I get up early, but I always go to bed early, too. I usually sleep for about eight hours.
P That's great, Marge. And now it's Robbie's turn. Robbie, how old are you?
R Twenty.
P And how often do you eat fast food?
R Well, I love pizza and hamburgers, and I sometimes have chips, so yeah, I eat fast food about five times a week.

P What about breakfast? How often do you have breakfast?
R I don't have time because I always get up late, so…I hardly ever have breakfast.
P OK, and how often do you do exercise?
R Oh, I do a lot of exercise. I play football four times a week.
P Good. That's better. And how many hours do you usually sleep?
R I'm not sure. I go to bed quite late because I'm on my computer, so I guess I sleep for about six hours.
P Right. Thank you, Robbie. And now it's time to see what the doctor thinks. Dr Atkins, Who's healthy? Marge? Robbie? Or both of them?
D Well, Marge always has breakfast and she never eats fast food. She often does exercise and she gets a lot of sleep. So, Marge, you're right. You're very healthy!
P And what about Robbie?
D Well, Robbie does exercise four times a week, but he often eats fast food and he never has breakfast. He doesn't sleep enough either. So Robbie, you're wrong. You aren't very healthy.
P So, there you have it everyone. A healthy mum and an unhealthy son! And that's all we have time for today. Join us again tomorrow at the same time for Who's healthy?

5 A

1 A Let's go to the swimming pool at the weekend.
  B OK. Can we go on Saturday? I'm busy on Sunday.
  A Yes, but I always play tennis in the morning. Let's go in the afternoon.
  B OK. See you there.
2 A I want to have lunch in this restaurant. Can I park here?
  B No, sir, you can't.
  A What about outside the cinema?
  B No parking spaces there. A lot of people leave their cars outside the hospital. You can park there.
  A Thanks.
3 A Can you help me with my homework?
  B Not now, sorry.
  A Can you help me after lunch?
  B No. I'm busy.
  A When can you help me?
  B After dinner. I don't have any plans tonight.
4 A Let's write a postcard to Chris. Do you have a pen?
  B Yes. Here you are.
  A What about a stamp?
  B We can buy a stamp in the shop.
  A Right. Do you know her address?
  B No. And you?
  A No, I don't!
5 A Right. Let's go in.
  B Sorry. We can't.
  A Why not? Are your parents home?
  B No, I can't hear them. But it isn't that. It's the door!
  A Oh, now I understand. You can't open it.
  B No! I don't know where my keys are!

5 B

Speaker 1 They both work, so it starts when they leave home in the morning. I don't know how many they have – three, four, five – but they make a terrible noise. They take them out for a walk in the evening, so it's nice and quiet then, but they sometimes go out at night and the noise starts again. I don't know why people have animals when they're never at home.

83

Speaker 2 It's really bad. They do it every Friday and Saturday night. The music starts at about eight o'clock and then we hear the cars. They park outside my house and soon the street is full of cars. The problem is that they don't stay in the house – they go out in the garden to dance, too. They don't leave until about six in the morning, so we don't sleep all night.

Speaker 3 They're really nice people, actually. He's a lawyer and she's a doctor. The problem is what they do in their free time. They both finish work early, so they're home by five o'clock. We can't watch TV or listen to our own music because we can't hear it. They play the piano and violin all evening. It's so noisy!

Speaker 4 I'm so tired at the moment. Every time I go to sleep, he starts… I know my neighbours love their son, and he's only three months old, but I wish he wouldn't wake up all the time. I thought babies sleep and eat all the time. He's changed my neighbours' lives, and he's changed mine too!

5 C))

Stop 1: Trinity College Dublin
The university and library were built in 1592. Famous students include writers and politicians. The most important book in the library is over a thousand years old.

Stop 2: The National Gallery
The gallery has more than 7,000 paintings and drawings by Irish and European artists. Some of the most famous works are by painters like Picasso, Goya, and Velázquez.

Stop 3: St Stephen's Green
The square is the biggest in Europe. It's a very quiet place with no cars. It has a lake where visitors can walk, and a place where you can listen to bands play many different types of music.

Stop 4: Dublin Castle
The castle you see now is not the original from 1204, but it is very important in the history of Ireland. The castle has some beautiful gardens.

Stop 5: Guinness Storehouse
The building is the home of the famous Irish beer, and the museum is part of the original factory. The exhibition shows how the workers make beer.

Stop 6: Kilmainham Gaol
This is a very famous prison from the past, but it has no prisoners now. The tour teaches visitors about the life of a prisoner in this cold, dark building.

Stop 7: Dublin Zoo
The zoo is in a very big park in the centre of the city. It's the third oldest zoo in the world, and the park is the largest park in any city in Europe. The most popular things to see at the zoo are the gorillas and chimpanzees.

Stop 8: Writer's museum
Dublin is the home of very famous writers like Oscar Wilde and James Joyce. The exhibition shows their books and letters in a beautiful big house that is 300 years old.

6 A))

H = Holly, B = Beth, E = Emily

H Hello, Emily. It's Holly.
B It isn't Emily. It's Beth. I'm Emily's sister.
H Oh. Hello. Um, is Emily there?
B No, I'm sorry. She's taking the dog for a walk.
H Oh. Well. Can you give her a message?
B Yes, of course.
H Can you tell her my bag is in her car and I need it?
B Oh. Your bag. Right. Does she have your number, Holly?
H I don't know.
B OK. Wait a minute. I need a pen. Right. What's your number?
H It's 60674 923.
B That's 60674 923.
H Yes, that's right.
B Wait a minute Holly. Don't go, I think Emily is opening the door. Emily? It's for you.
E What? Oh, the phone. Hello?
H Hi, Emily. It's Holly.
E Oh, hi, Holly. How are you?
H I'm fine. Listen. My bag's in your car.
E Is it?
H Yes. And my keys are in the bag, and I can't open the door of my flat. My mobile's in my bag too, so I'm calling from the flat next door. Can you give me my bag?
E Oh right. Yes. Yes, of course.
H Let's meet in the café near my house.
E Right. OK.
H Thanks, Emily.
E No problem. See you in a minute.
H Bye.

6 B))

Speaker 1 My favourite day of the year is New Year's Day. I always feel positive when I wake up and I love staying in bed for an hour or so, thinking about my plans for the next year. I like knowing that I can forget the disasters of the year before and just start again.

Speaker 2 I love waking up on the first day of my summer holiday. It's wonderful going somewhere new and you don't know anything about it. I don't like packing, though, so I always get my bags ready the night before. Then I can enjoy every second of my trip.

Speaker 3 My birthday is in autumn, which is probably why I love this season. I try to go out in the country at least once a week in autumn to see the beautiful colours of the trees. But I hate it when it rains and the leaves get wet and slippery!

Speaker 4 I hate being inside in the winter, especially when it gets dark at four o'clock, so I'm always waiting for spring to come. I love seeing the new spring flowers on one of those typical spring days, when it's cold but sunny. I love photography, and I often go out and take pictures of trees and flowers.

6 C))

1 A What kind of music do you like, Oliver?
  B I don't know. I like all kinds, really.
  A Well, do you like heavy metal?
  B Oh no! That's a bit loud for me.
  A What about reggae?
  B No. Reggae's a bit slow.
  A Well, what _do_ you like?
  B I usually listen to rock, so that's probably my favourite.
2 A Do you have a favourite CD?
  B Yes. Yes, I do. I always listen to it in the car.
  A Which group is it by?
  B Well, it's not really by a group. It's sung by actors.
  A Oh. Is it from a film?
  B Yes. It's the soundtrack from _Mamma Mia!_ I love it!
  A Isn't that about ABBA?
  B Yes and no…It's a musical, with the songs of ABBA, but the actors in the film sing them.
  A I see…

3 A How do you usually listen to music, Wendy?
  B Well, I don't listen to the radio, that's one thing for sure. I want to hear music, not the voices of the presenters.
  A What about CDs?
  B Well, I have quite a lot of those, but they're in a box in the garage somewhere. I usually listen to music on my laptop. I have a good internet connection at home and at work, and I can listen to what I want.
4 A Do you want to come to a concert next month?
  B OK. Who's playing? I hope it isn't Justin Bieber. You know I don't like him.
  A No, don't worry. This singer is nothing like him. Anyway, it's a woman.
  B Rihanna! Great! I'd love to come.
  A No, sorry, it isn't Rihanna. It's Beyoncé. They're quite similar, really.
  B Oh. Right. Beyoncé. OK. How much are the tickets?
5 A What do you think of this song, John?
  B I don't know. It's very different from her other songs.
  A I love it! It's really new and original.
  B Yes, but it's quite slow, and it isn't easy to dance to.
  A So you don't like it?
  B No, it's OK. But I prefer her other songs.

7 A))

P = Presenter, M = Mike

P Hello and welcome to what is a very special show, because we're going to find out the results of our poll. Mike Sandhurst from the BBC is here to tell us who is the greatest Briton of all time. Hello Mike.
M Hi there.
P So, let's look at the top five, Mike.
M All right. Well, number five on the list is, in fact, William Shakespeare.
P Really? I'm surprised.
M Me, too. Did you know that nobody knows his date of birth? Or that none of his plays were ever published when he was alive?
P No, I didn't know that! Very interesting and surprising! But who is number four?
M Well, number four is the scientist, Charles Darwin.
P Ah yes…Darwin. Tell us something about him.
M Well, he was born in Shrewsbury on 12th February, 1809. He was very interested in nature and animals and was responsible for the theory of evolution. He died in 1882 at the age of 73.
P OK. Who's next?
M Number three on the list is Diana, Princess of Wales.
P Yes, she was popular with a lot of people.
M That's right. So let me tell you about her. She was born on 1st July, 1961 in a village called Sandringham. She was famous because she was married to Prince Charles, but they weren't happy together and so they divorced. She died in a car crash in Paris in 1997. She was only 36 years old.
P Yes, that was a tragic accident. So, number two?
M Number two is the engineer Isambard Kingdom Brunel.
P Really? Tell us about him.
M Well, he was born on the 9th April, 1806 in Portsmouth. He was responsible for the first British railway, some big ships, and many important bridges and tunnels in Britain. He wasn't very old when he died, only 53.
P OK…and now for the moment we've been waiting for. Who is the greatest Briton of all time? Who is at the top of the list?

M Well, I'll give you a clue. It's a man…he was born on the 30th November, 1874, and died in 1965, He was a politician…and he was Prime Minister – not once, but twice.
P I knew it! It's Winston Churchill!
M That's right. Winston Churchill is the greatest Briton of all time.
P Mike Sandhurst, thank you so much for joining us.
M My pleasure.

7 B))

Speaker 1 I had a bad journey one Christmas when I wanted to visit my family back home in the UK. About twenty minutes after leaving the airport, there was a problem with our plane. We returned to the airport again and waited five hours for another plane. Finally, I arrived in the UK eight hours later than I planned.

Speaker 2 We tried to go on holiday to Portugal one year, but it was a disaster. We started our journey a bit late and stopped for lunch in a village on the way. When we were on the motorway after lunch, our car started making a strange noise and finally, it stopped altogether. The car ended up in a garage and we called a taxi to take us home again.

Speaker 3 My bad journey happened when I was at university. I wanted to go home for the weekend so I was on a train. The journey was very long – about seven hours – and I was nearly home. We stopped at the last station before mine, but then we didn't start again. The train was broken. In the end, my dad picked me up in his car.

Speaker 4 I had a bad experience with a bus company once. I booked a ticket from Victoria Bus Station to Stansted Airport but there were a lot of people at the bus station when I arrived, and it was impossible to get on the bus. In the end, I travelled to the airport with a businessman in a taxi. He didn't ask me for any money, which was nice.

7 C))

I = Interviewer, **H** = Helen
I Can you tell us about a memorable night, Helen?
H Well, let me see. There are quite a lot of them, actually. But yes, there was one particular night this year that was memorable.
I When was it?
H It was the 14th February.
I Valentine's Day?
H Yes. That's why I remember the date. It was Valentine's Day, but I didn't have a boyfriend at the time. In fact, I was with two friends.
I Where were you?
H I was in Manchester. There was a concert that night by my favourite band, Vampire Weekend, so I travelled to Manchester to see it.
I When did you arrive in Manchester?
H The night before the concert.
I So, what did you do before the concert?
H We had a drink in a very old pub in the city centre. Then we tried to find the concert. We didn't know exactly where the club was, so we walked around for a very long time. In the end, we got there five minutes before the concert started.
I Was the concert good?
H Yes, it was fantastic. The band played all our favourite songs, and we danced and sang for about two hours.
I Did you go home after the concert?
H No, we didn't go home straight away. We didn't have dinner before it started so we were hungry. We went to Manchester's Curry Mile and we had a curry. It was delicious! After that, we got a taxi home.
I What time did you get home?
H We didn't get home that late. It was two o'clock in the morning, more or less. But we had a great time. That was the important thing.

8 A))

P = Presenter, **D** = Detective
P Hello and welcome to What Next?, the programme that looks at today's career opportunities. In the studio with us is Chief Inspector Jeremy Downs from the Metropolitan Police. He's here to tell us a bit about his job and how he got it. Hello, Jeremy.
D Good morning, Peter.
P So, tell us, why did you decide to join the police?
D Well, it runs in my family, really. My dad was a detective, and so was his father. I always knew that this was what I wanted to do.
P What special qualifications did you need to become a detective?
D First, I had to get experience as a normal policeman. So I worked as a policeman for two years, and then I took a test called the National Investigators Exam. After that I did a course which was six weeks long, and then I began to work as a trainee investigator.
P Jeremy, what do you like most about your job?
D Well, you feel great when you solve a mystery and find a murderer. That's the best thing about it. And also, I'm usually outside or talking to people, so I don't spend much time in an office. I'm never bored when I'm working.
P And what don't you like about it?
D It's a very stressful job. I'm usually working on more than one case at a time, and sometimes it's difficult to know what to do first. And going to the scene of a murder can be terrible. But apart from that, I love my job and I recommend it to anyone who likes finding answers and solving problems.
P Chief Inspector Downs, thank you for joining us.

8 B))

M = Mrs Goodings, **J** = Joanna, **B** = Bradley
M Hello. Good morning. I'm Mrs Goodings.
J Hi. I'm Joanna, and this is Bradley.
B Hi.
M Hello. Please come in. So…let's start, shall we? This is the kitchen, as you can see.
B It's very big.
M Yes. There isn't a dining room, so we eat in here.
J Oh look! The walls are big windows! You can see the garden – it's beautiful!
B Can I ask you a question, Mrs Goodings? Why did we come in the back door?
M We always use the back door. There isn't a carpet in the kitchen so there aren't any problems with dirty shoes.
B Oh. Right.
J Where's the washing machine?
M It's in the corner over there.
J Oh, yes. I see it. Why is there a hole in the ceiling?
M Well, upstairs is the bathroom. The hole is for when you have a shower. You take off your clothes and put them down the hole. They land on the floor next to the washing machine.
J Oh. That's interesting!
M Yes…It was my idea…Now…this way please…I want to show you the living room. There. What do you think?
J Oh! There are big windows here, too. I love it!
B Mrs Goodings, is there a television?
M No, there isn't. My husband and I don't watch TV. We prefer listening to music. Now…let's go upstairs.
J There are four bedrooms upstairs, is that right?
M Yes. Four bedrooms and a bathroom.
B Is this the bathroom?
M Yes, it is. Be careful with the…
B Aargh!!!
J Bradley? Bradley? Where is he?
M Don't worry. He's in the kitchen.
J What?
M Do you remember the hole in the ceiling?
J Oh no! Bradley? Bradley? Are you all right?

8 C))

Speaker 1 When I was in Costa Rica, I stayed in a bed and breakfast hotel with a difference. It was in the middle of the jungle and we could see monkeys and birds from our window. As well as an air-conditioned bedroom, there was a full bathroom with a warm-water shower. We had a fridge and a coffee-maker, too.

Speaker 2 I spent the night in an ice hotel when I was in the North of Sweden. The temperature in the room was minus five degrees and the only furniture was a bed made of ice and snow. I slept in a special sleeping bag with all my clothes on – I even wore a hat! It wasn't very comfortable, really, because there wasn't even a bathroom!

Speaker 3 I once stayed in a very arty hotel when I was in Berlin. All of the rooms in the hotel were completely different. In the middle of my room there was a diamond-shaped bed and when I lay down, I could see hundreds of people who looked just like me. There weren't any cupboards, so I put my bags under the bed.

Speaker 4 I went to Fiji with my husband after we got married and we stayed in a really special hotel. A special lift took us down to our room, which was surrounded by fish and other sea animals. There was a large, comfortable bed in the bedroom and a library and personal office in the living room. We loved it there!

9 A))

Speaker 1 My favourite meal is roast beef. It sounds quite boring really – just a piece of meat, but you need to cook it for the right amount of time. My mum cooks it perfectly and she always serves it with roast potatoes and lots of other vegetables – peas, carrots, broccoli, and beans. Then she pours a sauce called gravy all over it. Delicious!

Speaker 2 Indian food is really popular in Britain these days, and I absolutely love it! We're lucky because we have a great Indian restaurant down the road. My favourite dish is chicken tikka masala, which is chicken in a sauce made with tomatoes, cream, and spices. I always order special Indian bread to eat with it.

Speaker 3 You probably think I'm mad, but one of my favourite meals is fish and chips. Yes, I know it's not very healthy, but I only have it about twice a month. I always buy it from the same shop and if the weather's nice, I sit outside in the park to eat it. I put lots of salt and vinegar on the chips. Yum!!!

Speaker 4 My favourite food is Chinese food and I always order the same dish – sweet and sour pork. This is bits of meat in a sauce made of sugar, tomatoes, white vinegar, and soy sauce. The sauce also has pineapple, green peppers, and onion in it. I always eat it with fried rice. I have it at the restaurant, and sometimes I get a takeaway and eat it at home.

9B

P = Presenter, **M** = Miriam

P Hello and welcome to the programme. Our first guest today is nutritionist Miriam Shepherd. She's here to give us some advice about healthy eating. Miriam, what do we need to eat to be healthy?
M Well, basically, we all need a balanced diet.
P And what exactly is a balanced diet?
M It's when you eat the right amount of food from each of the five different food groups.
P Can you tell us more about those groups, Miriam?
M Yes, of course. Let's start with carbohydrates. These are things like bread, pasta, rice, and potatoes. We need to eat a lot of carbohydrates because they give us energy.
P Right. What's next?
M The next group is fruit and vegetables. Things like apples and oranges, and peas and carrots. These contain important vitamins so you need to eat something from this group at every meal.
P OK. What the third group?
M The third group is protein, which is in food like meat and eggs. We need it to grow and to repair the body. You need to eat quite a lot of foods from this group, but not necessarily with every meal.
P Right. What's the next group, Miriam?
M Milk and dairy. Dairy foods are things like cheese and yoghurt. This group contains calcium which is important for our bones and teeth. But you have to be a little careful because they sometimes contain a lot of fat. You need to eat something from this group every day, but not necessarily every meal.
P And which is the last group, Miriam?
M The last group is fats and sugars. These are found in snacks, like cakes, biscuits, sweets, and crisps. Fats and sugars aren't very good for you, so only eat a little food from this group – maybe once or twice a week.
P Thank you, Miriam. That was very helpful.
M My pleasure.

9C

M = Michael, **R** = Rachel

M Rachel, did you know that there are two cities called Birmingham?
R Really? I know the one in the UK, but where's the other one?
M It's in the USA, in the state of Alabama.
R OK. Are the cities very small?
M Not really. One big difference is the population. There are only 243,000 people living in Birmingham USA, whereas there are over a million in Birmingham UK.
R So, Birmingham UK is bigger then?
M Well, no. The area of Birmingham UK is 165 square kilometres while Birmingham USA covers 243 square kilometres.
R Oh, that's quite big.
M Yes, but there aren't as many people. Birmingham USA is also very green.
R And our Birmingham isn't very green.
M Yes. And of course there's also a big difference in age. Birmingham, UK was already a small village as early as the seventh century while Birmingham USA didn't exist until 1871.
R Right. What about the weather? It's always raining over here so the weather is probably better in Birmingham USA.
M No, you're wrong. There are 1,371 millimetres of rain in Birmingham USA and only half of that in Birmingham UK – 662 millimetres.
R Wow! That's a surprise!
M Yes, but it's hotter over there. The average temperature in Birmingham UK is only 13 degrees whereas in Birmingham USA it's 23 degrees. That's ten degrees warmer.
R So, why are you telling me all this anyway?
M I'm reading an article in the newspaper. It's about a mistake that they made in Birmingham. That's our Birmingham, not theirs.
R What happened?
M They made an advert for Birmingham UK, but they used the wrong photo. They put a photo of Birmingham USA on the advert instead of Birmingham UK.
R No! How funny!
M Yes, I thought so, too!

10A

P = Presenter, **H** = Harry

P Hello and welcome to the travel section of the programme. Our guest today is travel writer Harry Miller, whose book *Superlative Sights* came out yesterday. Harry, welcome to the programme.
H Thank you, Gloria.
P So what exactly is your book about?
H Well, it's basically about the biggest, the best and the most beautiful places in the world.
P Can you give us some examples?
H Yes, of course. Let's start with Ayers Rock in Australia. Its other name is Uluru and it's the world's largest rock. It's 3.6 kilometres long, 2 kilometres wide and 348 metres high – enormous!
P Yes, I see what you mean. What else?
H How about the world's highest waterfall? The Angel Falls in Venezuela are 979 metres high. A lot of the water evaporates before it hits the ground.
P Wow! Are there only natural places in your book, or do you have any man-made structures?
H Yes, we include man-made structures too. For example, do you know what the tallest building is right now?
P No…tell us more.
H Well, it's Burj Khalifa in Dubai in the United Arab Emirates. It stands 828 metres high.
P Incredible!
H What about the oldest city in the world?
P I'm not sure. Um…somewhere in Egypt?
H Nearly, but not quite. It's Aleppo, in Syria. The city dates back to 600 BC and it's the oldest continuously inhabited city in the world.
P Really? I didn't know that.
H There are also some interesting facts about transport. For instance, do you know anything about the longest railway journey?
P Well, I suppose it's in Russia.
H That's right. The Trans-Siberian Railway from Moscow to Vladivostok is 9,297 kilometres long and crosses seven different time zones.
P That's one long train ride!
H That's right. And how about plane journeys? What's the shortest runway in the world?
P Runway? You mean where the planes land at the airport?
H That's right.
P I have no idea.
H Well, it's on the beautiful island of Saba in the Dutch Caribbean. The runway is only 400 metres long and it ends in a 60-metre drop into the sea.
P This is fascinating stuff Harry. I can't wait to read your book!

10B

Speaker 1 I had my first experience of CouchSurfing in China. I wanted to spend a few days in a city called Guilin so I made contact with a Chinese guy called Leo. Leo was the perfect host: he gave me a bed, he organized a dinner that other CouchSurfers came to, and he showed me around the city. I loved it, and I'd recommend it to anyone!

Speaker 2 My first CouchSurfing experience did not go well. I was in Bucharest, Romania, and I found an American guy who agreed to host me. First he was late and then he didn't stop talking about himself all night. In the end, I said I was tired and went to bed. The next morning, I left Bucharest and took the train to Transylvania, where my host was Romanian and I had a much better time.

Speaker 3 I'm American and my first CouchSurfing experience was in England. I wanted to do some research for a novel I'm writing, so I needed to meet as many people as possible. My sister told me about the website so I decided to try it out. In the end, I stayed with someone different every night and I got a lot of ideas for my book!

Speaker 4 I was in Australia working when I found out about the CouchSurfing website. I wanted to travel around the country at weekends, but I didn't know anyone. A friend suggested looking at the CouchSurfing website and I'm very happy that I did. I now have friends all over Australia and some of them are going to visit me in the USA when I go back next month.

10C

P = Pete, **A** = Amy

P Amy, do you remember Uri Geller?
A No, I don't. Who was he?
P He was a kind of psychic. He was on TV a lot in the past and he became quite famous.
A What kind of tricks did he do?
P Well, his most famous trick was bending spoons. There's a photo here – come and have a look.
A Oh, there's a video here too on YouTube. Let's watch it.
P You see? At first, the spoon looks normal. Here, he's touching it with his finger…and now, it's bent.
A That's amazing!
P Actually…it isn't.
A What?
P It's a trick.
A So how does he do it?
P The spoon is bent before he shows it to us. He's hiding the bent part in his hand, so that you think it's a normal spoon. You don't have much time to look at the spoon at all because he's talking so much. What he's doing is distracting you while he's pulling the bent spoon slowly out of his hand. You think he's bending it but, in fact, he isn't.
A So, the guy is a cheat!
P Yes, but he's a very famous cheat.
A Does he still do his trick in public?
P Yes, he does. And the most incredible thing is that people still believe it.

11A

Speaker 1: Brno, Czech Republic
At the weekend, the city is really quiet, which is a surprise because there are many university students. A lot of people go to the country, to spend time with their families in their country cottages. I think family is very important to Czech people,

which is really nice but it also means that the cities are almost empty at the weekends.

People dress very casually here, especially at work. In big companies, it's quite normal to wear jeans and T-shirts, even for managers and directors. The only time I've seen Czech people wear suits or smart clothes is to go to the theatre.

An interesting thing is that there are lots of shops under the street. You can buy all sorts of things here: food, clothes, books, everything really. They're little shops, and often cheaper than the bigger international shops in the main shopping areas. I think they're under the street because it's so cold in winter.

Speaker 2: Reykjavik, Iceland
In Iceland, a very important part of life is swimming and going to a hot tub, which is like a small swimming pool with hot water. People go before work or at the weekend to meet with their friends, or sometimes even to have business meetings!

The countryside in Iceland in incredible. There are almost no trees, and there are volcanoes and fields of lava, which are the incredibly hot stones which come out of the volcanoes. You can walk for days and not see another person, because there aren't many people in Iceland. In Reykjavik, there are fewer than 250,000, and the second-biggest city has only 15,000 people.

Icelandic people are very creative. It's normal for many people to make music, paint or draw, and even write books. Also, many people make their own clothes, and they look really fashionable!

11 B))

P = Presenter, **D** = Dave, **S** = Sandy, **E** = Eddie
P Hello. I'm Jenny Richards and I'm out on the streets of Birmingham asking people what they want to do with their lives. Let's start with this man over here. Hello.
D Hi.
P I'm Jenny Richards from Central TV. What's your name?
D I'm Dave.
P Right, Dave, we'd like to ask you about your ambitions for the future. What do you want to do with your life?
D Well, er, what I'd really like, um, is…
P Yes?
D I'd really like to buy a motorbike. I had a little Vespa when I was younger but I stopped riding it when I got married and had kids. Now, I'd like to start again.
P Well, good luck with your ambition, Dave. Let's talk to someone else now. Hello. What's your name?
S Sandy.
P So, what do you want to do with your life, Sandy?
S Well, I'd love to go travelling to different places.
P Oh really? Any particular place?
S Yes. I'd really like to go to Australia with my boyfriend. I have family there and it's a very exciting country.
P Why don't you, then?
S I can't.
P Why not?
S My boyfriend hates flying, and it's a 22-hour flight.
P Well, maybe one day you can go there on your own. Good luck with your ambition, Sandy. Now, what about you? What's your name?
E I'm Eddie.
P Do you have any ambitions Eddie?
E I'd like to see Kings of Leon live.
P Why Kings of Leon?
E They're my favourite band.
P Why don't you get a ticket for their next concert?
E Yeah, I want to but they aren't touring this year. They're making a new album.
P Well maybe next year. Now let's talk to this woman over here…

11 C))

Speaker 1 I really couldn't live without the internet. Every evening after dinner, I spend a few hours on my laptop playing games online. My job is very stressful, so it helps me relax. I forget about my problems and focus on something different. I think it's really good for me.
Speaker 2 The internet is really important for me because I live abroad. All of my family and friends live in the UK and I'm living in New York. Phone calls are really expensive, but with the internet I can Skype them whenever I want to. With Skype I can even see their faces, so it's much better than a phone call.
Speaker 3 Well, um, I'm a webmaster, so the internet is very important for my job. I work with different websites, first of all creating them and then making sure that everyone can use them. I also try to make existing websites work faster. I enjoy my job because I love computers and solving problems.
Speaker 4 Yeah, I spend quite a lot of time on the internet every day. It's a great way to keep in touch with friends, and also to meet new people. There's one site I use a lot to chat with my friends, upload photos and post videos that I find funny. I also like looking at my friends' profiles to see what they're doing.

12 A))

P = Presenter, **C** = Christopher
P Hello and welcome to Focus on Film. In the studio with us today is film critic Christopher Phillips. We've asked him to choose his two favourite film adaptations of books. Christopher, where are you going to start?
C Well, it's been a difficult choice but I'm going to start with a very early film, the 1946 adaptation of *Great Expectations* by Charles Dickens.
P 1946? That is early.
C Yes, and as you can imagine, the film is in black and white. It tells the story of a poor young boy called Pip who, with the help of a mysterious person, becomes a gentleman. The story doesn't change much in the film, but the photography makes the atmosphere darker and more frightening. It's an excellent adaptation.
P *Great Expectations*. Right. I haven't seen the film, but I've read the book, of course. What's your other film, Christopher?
C Well, my other choice is a bit more recent. It's *The English Patient*.
P Yes, I've seen that one a few times. But I don't know anything about the book. Tell us more.
C Well, the author is a Sri Lankan-Canadian writer called Michael Ondaatje and his novel won an important prize – the Booker Prize. The film came out in 1996 and it's a wonderful adaptation of the book. It tells the story of a man in a military hospital who has been in a plane crash. We also learn something about the life and loves of his nurse. Again there are few changes to the story, but the best thing about the film is the choice of actors, who are perfect for their parts. The film won a total of nine Oscars, which shows just how good it is.
P Christopher Phillips, thank you for joining us.
C Thank you for having me. I've enjoyed it.

12 B))

Speaker 1 **I** = Interviewer, **S** = Speaker 1
I Have you ever been to Africa?
S Yes, I have. I've been to Kenya.
I When did you go?
S I went in 2010. We stayed with some friends who are living in Nairobi. While we were there, we went on a trip to Tsavo East, which is an enormous national park. It's as big as Wales. Unfortunately, our car broke down in the park and the guards took six hours to rescue us. It was quite frightening!
Speaker 2 **I** = Interviewer, **S** = Speaker 2
I Have you ever been to South America?
S Yes, I have. I've been to Brazil.
I When did you go?
S I went there in 2006 on a business trip. In fact, we were at a conference so it wasn't very hard work. We stayed in a five-star hotel and the company paid for everything.
Speaker 3 **I** = Interviewer, **S** = Speaker 3
I Have you ever been to Australia?
S Well, I haven't been to Australia, but I've been to New Zealand.
I When did you go?
S I went with my wife when we got married in 2011. We stayed in a luxury apartment on the banks of Lake Wakatipu and we had a great time doing lots of different water sports. The best moment for me, though, was when we did a bungee jump from the Kawarau Bridge. It was really exciting!
Speaker 4 **I** = Interviewer, **S** = Speaker 4
I Have you ever been to Asia?
S Yes, I have. I've been to Thailand.
I When did you go?
S I went with my family in Easter, 2006. We stayed in a special hotel in the jungle and we slept in a treehouse. But the most amazing part of our trip happened when we visited Bangkok. We were lucky enough to be there for Songkran, the Thai New Year, so we saw the water festival. You know, the one where everybody throws water at each other in the street!

12 C))

New Zealand. Home of Middle Earth. And the best way to experience it is on our *Lord of the Rings* Edoras tour. The tour leaves Christchurch at nine a.m. and returns at six p.m. but we can pick you up at other central city locations, too. The groups are small, and the guides are friendly and informative. You don't need to be a *Lord of the Rings* fan to enjoy the tour as the scenery is fantastic. Transport is in a Land Rover, and we take you through the spectacular mountains of the Southern Alps where you can see clear lakes and blue rivers and you can breathe fresh mountain air. Our destination is Mount Sunday, the real-life mountain which in the film is Edoras, the capital city of the Rohan people. While you're there, you can use some the most famous items from the film: Aragorn's sword, Gimli's axe and the flag of Rohan. For lunch there is a luxury picnic, which we eat outside in the open air. Visit our shop at the end or your trip and buy exclusive Lord of the Rings souvenirs for your family and friends back home.

The tour runs daily throughout the year and you can buy tickets online. The price includes your pick up and drop off, your journey in the Land Rover, your guided walk to the very top of Edoras, and your delicious lunch. Tickets cost $135 for adults, per person, and $94 for children aged 14 and under.

So, what are you waiting for? Book your tickets now before you miss your chance to see one of the most beautiful *Lord of the Rings* locations. It's an experience you'll never forget.

Great Clarendon Street, Oxford, OX2 6DP, United Kingdom

Oxford University Press is a department of the University of Oxford.
It furthers the University's objective of excellence in research, scholarship,
and education by publishing worldwide. Oxford is a registered trade
mark of Oxford University Press in the UK and in certain other countries

© Oxford University Press 2012

The moral rights of the author have been asserted

First published in 2012

2016 2015 2014 2013 2012

10 9 8 7 6 5 4 3 2 1

No unauthorized photocopying

All rights reserved. No part of this publication may be reproduced, stored
in a retrieval system, or transmitted, in any form or by any means, without
the prior permission in writing of Oxford University Press, or as expressly
permitted by law, by licence or under terms agreed with the appropriate
reprographics rights organization. Enquiries concerning reproduction outside
the scope of the above should be sent to the ELT Rights Department, Oxford
University Press, at the address above

You must not circulate this work in any other form and you must impose
this same condition on any acquirer

Links to third party websites are provided by Oxford in good faith and for
information only. Oxford disclaims any responsibility for the materials
contained in any third party website referenced in this work

ISBN: 978 0 19 459819 4

Printed and bound by Gráfica Maiadouro S.A. in Portugal

This book is printed on paper from certified and well-managed sources

ACKNOWLEDGEMENTS

The authors would like to thank all the teachers and students round the world whose feedback has helped us to shape English File.

The authors would also like to thank: all those at Oxford University Press (both in Oxford and around the world) and the design team who have contributed their skills and ideas to producing this course.

Finally very special thanks from Clive to Maria Angeles, Lucia, and Eric, and from Christina to Cristina, for all their support and encouragement. Christina would also like to thank her children Joaquin, Marco, and Krysia for their constant inspiration.

The authors and publisher are grateful to those who have given permission to reproduce the following extracts and adaptations of copyright material: p.38 Extract from Oxford Bookworms Library Starter: *Sally's Phone* by Christine Lindop © Oxford University Press 2007. Reproduced by Permission; p.81 Extract from 'Lord of the Rings – New Zealand', from http://www.tourism.net.nz. Reproduced by permission of New Zealand Tourism Guide.

Sources: p.77 http://blog.moviefone.com; p.81 http://www.hasslefree.co.nz

The publishers would like to thank the following for their kind permission to reproduce photographs: Alamy Images pp.10 (Sheraton Skyline Hotel/Michael Rose), 10 (The Grove Hotel/Chris Ferris), 12 (laptop case/Richard Heyes), 12 (red rucksack/D. Hurst), 11 (wallet/L A Heukisinkveld), 11 (newspaper/Geoffrey Kidd), 11 (ticket/Kevin Wheal), 12 (tourist bag/Jason Batterham), 18 (woman smiling/ImageState), 19 (shop assistant/AceStock ltd), 22 (couple having dinner/Christophe Viseux), 22 (facebook logo/digitallife), 23 (Edinburgh, Scotland/ilpo musto), 26 (man smiling/Yuri Arcurs), 28 (woman with a Cold/Michael AKeller), 31 (singing/Image Source), 31 (drawing/Shepic), 34 (Mousa ferry/Vincent Lowe), 34 (Cloudy summer sky/Stefan Sollfors), 35 (Salisbury Crags/Daivd Lyons), 36 (John Lewis Store/Greg Balfour Evans), 41 (Johann Sebastian Bach/Lebrecht Music and Arts Photo Library), 41 (Beethoven/GL Archive), 49 (coach/Justin Kase ztwoz), 49 (Virgin train/Matthew Clarke), 49 (driving on the A66 route/incamerastock), 51 (magnifying glass/Radius Images), 57 (ice lolly/Lucie Lang), 64 (mosque/Paul Doyle), 64 (police station/Justin Kase ztwoz), 64 (theatre/Kirsty McLaren), 64 (bridge/Motoring Picture Library), 64 (arcade/David Bagnall), 64 (Paternoster Square/Peter Crome), 64 (town hall/Les Ladbury), 64 (market/Homer Sykes), 64 (church/incamerastock), 64 (Bodiam Castle/BL Images), 68 (bent spoon/Anna Idestam-Almquist), 70 (rooftops/Gavin Hellier), 70 (Reykjavik/Gavin Hellier), 74 (optical fibres/Photo Provider Network), 81 (New Zealand/Stuart Barry); Corbis pp.19 (engineer/Andrew Brookes), 19 (production line/Monty Rakusen/Cultura), 11 (architect/Rick Gomez), 19 (dentist/Benelux), 22 (teenage girls on mobile phones/JGI/Jamie Grill/Blend Images), 24 (elderly woman/Radius Images), 26 (smiling woman/A&Me/Johnér Images), 28 (jogging/Tetra Images), 29 (elderly lady/Tom Stewart), 31 (swimming/Fran and Helena/Culture), 31 (whispering), 34 (running/Jose Luis Pelaez, Inc), 31 (tango/Jim Naughten), 34 (fog/Image Source), 34 (beach/Mike Theiss), 34 (snow/Paul Burns), 34 (storm/Carl Purcell), 35 (Princes Street in Edinburgh/Douglas Pearson), 44 (Composer Benjamin Britten/BBC), 44 (Shakespeare/Bettmann), 44 (Princess Diana/David Levinson), 44 (Winston Churchill/Corbis), 44 (Charles Darwin/Bettmann), 47 (couple/Wavebreak Media Ltd), 48 (coffee shop/Beau Lark), 54 (turtles/Paulo Whitaker), 65 (girls/Jutta Klee), 72 (businesswoman/Jose Luis Pelaez); Corbis Images p.79 (Schonbrunn Palace/Rudy Sulgan); Flicker p.55 (Maesmawr Hall Hotel/Karen Blakeman); Getty Images pp.7 (boy with notebook/zhang bo), 19 (vet/Malcolm MacGregor), 19 (model/Stefan Gosatti), 31 (having coffee/Ghislain and Marie David de Lossy), (at bus stop/Photolibrary), 31 (thoughtful man/Photolibrary/Fancy), 31 (giving flowers/Photolibrary/Fancy), 31 (painting/Mark Romanelli), 31 (computer(Digital Vision), 31 (driving/Photolibrary), 31 (taking photo/Oliver Rossi), 33 (man/John Giustina), 34 (Savannah sunset/Pete Turner), 35 (Edinburgh castle/Fraser Hall), 37 (mobile phone/James Whitaker), 41 (Iron Maiden/Steve Thorne), 43 (Jane Austen/Stock Montage), 44 (Brunel/Hulton Archive/Stringer), 46 (tennis/Julian Finney), 57 (Green Coconut/Richard Watson), 59 (food groups/Michael Rosenfeld); Image Source pp.26 (man/Image source), 39 (man smiling/Camarena), 72 (boy/Image source); iStockphoto p.73 (internet connection/ahlobystov); Kobal Collection pp.77 (*My Sisters Keeper* Poster/Mark Johnson Productions), 81 (*Lord Of The Rings* Poster/New Line/Saul Zaentz/Wing Nut); Oxford University Press pp.7 (teacher/Image Source), 7 (phone/Cultura), 9 (soldier/Photodisc), 12 (handbag/Dennis Kitchen Studio, Inc), 18 (woman/Image Source), 18 (office worker/Image Source), 19 (chef/Tetra Images), 24 (elderly man/Johner Images), 27 (taxi/Digital Vision), 31 (at cinema/Image Source), 39 (woman/Image Source), 57 (camel/Photodisc), 72 (man/Digital Vision); Rex Features pp.14 (Walk of Fame/Foubert), 41 (Rihanna performs/Picture Perfect), 41 (Concert NBCU Photobank/Rex Features.), 41 (BBC Radio 1's Big Weekend 2011 festival/Brian Rasic/Rex Features), 41 (John Lee Hooker/Rex Features), 41 (Jennifer Lopez/BDG/Rex Features), 41 (Reggae Bash/Sipa Press), 41 (Jamie Cullum/Isopix), 64 (museum/BananaStock).

Illustrations by: Peter Bull p.49; Clive Goodyer pp.8, 15, 20, 50, 52, 69; Atushi Hara/DutchUncleagency pp.4, 5, 58, 67; Sophie Joyce pp.11, 12; Tim Marrs pp.61; Jerome Mirault/Colagene p.13; Roger Penwill pp.30, 33, 54.

Commissioned photography by: MM Studios p.11 (apart from frames 2, 4, 7), p.56

Designed by: Stephen Strong